THE

BREAKNECK HAMLET

COMPANION

An Actor's Notebook

THE

BREAKNECK HAMLET

COMPANION

An Actor's Notebook

Featuring the complete text, recklessly sliced from William Shakespeare's "Hamlet"
Adapted, Edited, and Explained…

by Timothy Mooney

THE BREAKNECK HAMLET COMPANION; AN ACTOR'S NOTEBOOK
© 2015 by Timothy Mooney

ALL RIGHTS RESERVED

Credits:
Cover Illustration by David S. Jensen
Cover Photo by Brian McConkey

ISBN 13: 978-0-9831812-5-5
ISBN 10: 0-9831812-5-5
LCCN: 2015911024

Reviews of Breakneck Hamlet!

It's a madcap, high-energy and both funny and affecting take… delighting in Shakespeare's witty wordplay… This is the way Shakespeare should be taught—heard, lived, experienced… And Mooney brings it together with tremendous passion and way more energy than any one man ought to possess.

Allison Carter, IndyStar.com

[Mooney] gives prominence to the recurring themes so much so that it's as if they are lit up in neon lights… a whirlwind of wonderful. Hold on to your seats and watch a master at his work. *Lee Hartman, KCMetropolis.org*

Must See: What an hour it is!… Audiences will still come away with a thorough understanding of it and get a few laughs along the way… *Breakneck Hamlet* is truly breakneck, and may leave you panting with exertion as Mooney goes through his paces. *Maren Longbella, Twin Cities Pioneer Press*

Brilliant… [Mooney] knows his Shakespeare forwards, backwards and out-of-context… He seamlessly throws in asides, explanations and famous lines as he whirls to the play's conclusion. *Jodie Jacobs, Examiner.com*

Succinct and engaging… animated and eloquent. *Deborah Hirsch, The Pitch*

I've seen *Hamlet* more than any other Shakespeare play, and yet I feel like I've gained new insights… Timothy is a charming host with much energy, excitement, physicality… You've probably seen *Hamlet* before, but you've never seen *Hamlet* quite like this. *Jill Schafer, Cherryandspoon.com*

Astonishing… a concise cliff-hanger… Gestures are precise, elaborate and underlined by stark changes in vocal tone… an assured and lively adaptation.

Jay Harvey, jayharveyupstage.blogspot.com

At the speed of sound, he seamlessly summarizes important plot points [and] perform selected scenes with gusto. It runs rings around that other performance by Mel Gibson. *Dan Grossman, Nuvo Magazine*

Fun, Fearless Shakespeare… Cliff Notes on caffeine.

Cora Vasseur, Halfstack Magazine

A rollicking version… such passion and skill that you will wonder why this is not the standard presentation of the show. If all of Shakespeare's works were taught like this in schools, students would embrace the works delightedly.

Wendy Carson, "Plays with John & Wendy"

Audience Response to Breakneck Hamlet!

Yes, it is all the best of this best of all plays.   *Debra Ann Christensen*

Everything we need to enjoy this masterpiece in one-third of the time.
     Kate Hutchinson, veteran high school A. P. English teacher

Tim's talent breaks through the most intimidating aspect of Shakespeare—the unfamiliar language—and makes it crystal-clear.   *Donna Yarborough*

One actor with an empty stage and two props will knock your socks off.
     Mariellen Jacobson

Never have I been taken through complexity so fast and yet so clearly. There were points about *Hamlet* I understood for the first time.   *Harriet McCleary*

Most insightful and fun look at Shakespeare since… well… Shakespeare!
     Kevin Holladay, Schedule C Shows

AN EXPLOSION OF CLARITY! Tim Mooney's one-man interpretation made Shakespeare come alive before my eyes. I finally understand *Hamlet*!
     Bob Weidman

Who knew you could cut Hamlet down to a one-man, 60-minute show and have an avid Shakespeare-fan still LOVE it??   *Hannah May, @hmay1023*

He charges through a 4-hour play in one hour, all while putting *Hamlet* in its correct historical context and showing all the political machinations that have made *Hamlet* perhaps the greatest play of all time.   *Kale Ganann*

Luminous linguistic beauty… theatrically accessible, remarkably clear, and vibrantly alive.   *Robert Hubbard*

Clever, classy and kaleidoscopic with humor… will spin the dust off the story for the most resistant student of Shakespeare.   *Anthony Logan Nathan*

Creepy as hell, hysterically funny and horribly tragic…!   *Marie Cooney*

Tim's asides be mirthful yet unforced; his energy like a monsoon; his acting clear & stellar; & best of all, his unique narration doth illuminate the story such that even I—Hamlet-soaked for nigh 3 decades—didst see things I had not seen afore now, & I LEARNED ANEW. The rest is silence. *Amy Salloway*

Reviews of Tim's first "Breakneck Shakespeare" work:
Shakespeare's Histories; *Ten Epic Plays at a Breakneck Pace!*

Shakespeare's Histories, The Book…

Dazzling, robust, dedicated, and nothing short of brilliant artistry… comparable to Carl Sagan's interpretation of the Cosmos. Only faster, and funnier. *Eduardo Santiago, Award-winning Author of Midnight Rumba*

A really excellent distillation of very complex history… Would make a great companion piece to any season that's doing one of the histories… *Christina Gutierrez, Producing Artistic Director, 7 Towers Theatre*

An invaluable text for actors studying period styles, students in my Theater and Drama Appreciation course, or in my Introduction to Shakespeare literature course… with penetrating insight into language, character, thought, and action… If students can have only one Shakespeare book in their libraries to add depth to their understanding of these history plays--make it this one! *Rick Plummer, Arts & Humanities Chair, West Shore Community College*

A slim volume of clear, accessible explanations of the history behind Shakespeare's plays. A dizzying performance text… This is the most fun you'll ever have preparing for *Richard III*. *Eileen Polk, The Tudor Guild*

Accessible and immensely enjoyable, the implications for lesson plans and cross-disciplines of drama, speech, and English are limitless… For the novice performer or the well-informed scholar, a must-read/must-own addition. *Aaron Adair, PhD, Assistant Dean, Southeastern Oklahoma University*

An absolutely wonderful new approach… I will be incorporating this in any Shakespeare or Dramatic Literature class I'll be teaching… a delight even to those already familiar. *Melissa Berry, Mount St. Mary's College, Los Angeles*

Shakespeare's Histories is fantastic because it highlights how *insanely* important the rights of succession were and helps bring an understanding of this very alien concept to Americans. Which ultimately, helps all these plays make more sense. *Kate Mura, Artistic Ambassador, Fuse Theatre Ensemble*

I was delighted to pick up *Richard II* right after finishing Tim Mooney's book, read the list of characters and find them clicking into place in my head, their personalities and motives all fleshed out… I finished *Richard II* in an evening (and loved it), and I'm now eager to tackle the rest… a fast, engaging and often irreverent guide to the history plays… a rollicking good time. *Felicia Jordan*

Reviews of "Shakespeare's Histories," the Show...

Mooney connects the dots between the plays, reveals the author's liberties with factual events, and his penchant for having his reality-based characters wildly prophesying on anything and everything... Mooney [points] out ironies and discrepancies with enthusiasm and determination... There is a staggering amount of material—war, murder, deception, banishment, conquests, family drama, and much more. Mooney makes it accessible, enjoyable, and fun.
Kristin Shafel Omiccioli, KCMetropolis.org

Colorful and concise [combining] famous Shakespeare text with an animated CliffsNotes take on English royal lineage that transfix, leaving you entertained and feeling smarter. *Liz Cook & Deborah Hirsch, The Pitch.com*

Timothy Mooney takes us through the War of the Roses, the Hundred Years War, treason, madness, France conquered, France lost, Henries, Richards, Edwards, and some of the greatest speeches in the history of the English language with charm and clarifying wit... The great, grand picture of the wars of English succession will fill itself in your mind more complete than ever. Think of this as a jumping off point: a quick jump-start in a lifelong love of some of the greatest plays ever written. *Kelly Luck, KCStage.com*

Spookily impressive... like attending one of the most entertaining college-level English lectures ever... a torrent of knowledge... A do-not-miss show...
Jessica Bryce Young, Orlando Weekly

If only cramming for an exam were as enjoyable... It's an epic in an hour... 10 plays about seven kings and 23 distinct characters, each employing Shakespeare's sumptuously poetic words... It's best when the exhaustingly energetic Mooney introduces you to rich, complex characters like the existentially conflicted Richard II or Joan of Arc as seen through Elizabethan eyes (the little witch). Mooney brings welcome clarity to what all those wars and words were about. *Rob Hubbard, Pioneer Press*

An awesome thing to see, in the sense that it will fill you with awe — awe that one person can not only remember all those names, dates, and details, but that he can also remember all those Shakespearean speeches, the different mannerisms and voices for each character, and make it all interesting... Mooney makes sharp, witty insights into Shakespeare's choices [and] truly brings the stories to life. *Liz Byron, Aisle Say Twin Cities*

Mooney is the English teacher you always wish you had... This is all the stuff that would be 3 credit hours in an English lit program, but this show is quicker, more fun, and doesn't have that nasty midterm theme paper due.
Carl F. Gauze, Ink19.com

ABOUT THE ADAPTOR/EDITOR/EXPLAINER:

Timothy Mooney has adapted seventeen of Molière's plays to the stage, seen in the United States, and around the world, many of them published by Playscripts, Inc. Tim's latest, a rhymed version of Goldoni's *Servant of Two Masters* premiered at the Annapolis Shakespeare Festival in the summer of 2015. His one-man plays, *Molière than Thou, Lot o' Shakespeare* and *Shakespeare's Histories; Ten Epic Plays at a Breakneck Pace!* are turning a new generation on to Molière and Shakespeare, while Mooney's *The Greatest Speech of All Time* recreates actual historical speeches ranging from Socrates to Martin Luther King Jr.

Previously, Tim taught acting at Northern Illinois University, and published his own newsletter, *The Script Review*. As Artistic Director of the Stage Two Theatre, Tim produced nearly fifty plays in five years. Inaugurating the *TMRT Press* in 2011 with his long-awaited acting text, *Acting at the Speed of Life; Conquering Theatrical Style*, Tim followed up with *The Big Book of Molière Monologues* before releasing parts of his one-man catalogue into published form, beginning with *Molière Than Thou* and *Criteria, a One-Man Comic Sci-Fi Thriller!* Last year's release, *Shakespeare's Histories; Ten Epic Plays at a Breakneck Pace!* initiated Tim's new brand… "Breakneck Shakespeare!"

DEDICATION:

To Thomas Hauger, the charming, gracious and generous Norwegian, who envisioned and believed in me doing this play, before I even imagined it!

SPECIAL THANKS:

To Deb Pekin, April Peterson, Bob Sanders, Sabrina Wottreng and the 150 contributors to the "*Breakneck Hamlet* Indiegogo Campaign," who made this show possible!

From the Adaptor/Editor/Explainer…

It seems most of my one-man show ideas are outgrowths of previous one-man shows…

In 1999, I wrote and memorized *Molière than Thou*, which has kind-of been my bread and butter for the last 15 years.

I tested the waters with a few other one-man shows, including the still-popular *Criteria, a One-Man Comic Sci-Fi Thriller*, but returned to what has become my "classical theatre brand" with *Lot o' Shakespeare*, which featured one monologue from every Shakespeare play, selected randomly, "bingo style."

As a mostly-comic actor who judges his own value by how many laughs he gets in a given evening, I was shocked to discover that some of my most popular pieces in "*LoS*" (such as Mark Antony & Henry V) were not really comic at all! Seeing just how moved the audiences were by the amazing rhetoric of those speeches, I assembled a collection of actual historical speeches, *The Greatest Speech of All Time*, to get at the question of "What is this thing called rhetoric?" and "Just what makes a great speech anyway?"

Also branching off from the rich vein that *Lot o' Shakespeare* had mined, I developed *Shakespeare's Histories; Ten Epic Plays at a Breakneck Pace*, in order to reflect the chronology of those history plays in such a way that the modern American mind could understand and absorb them, perhaps to make them available to a culture not fully steeped in the history that any Elizabethan schoolchild would have already known.

Last summer, performing *Shakespeare's Histories* as a last minute replacement at an international theatre festival (the group from Togo was a no-show), an adjudicator from Denmark was particularly enthusiastic. He came up to me after the show to tell me how much he had enjoyed it, and also to suggest…

"It was great, but I really wish that you could do this kind of a treatment for a single play, so that you could dive in deeper and really reveal the characters."

"Hmm. That sounds exciting. What play do you think I ought to take on?"

"Well… I'm from Denmark…"

I was very touched by this, although *Hamlet* had never quite been my favorite Shakespeare play. I was particularly fond of *King Lear*, and flirted with the idea of what a one-man *King Lear* would look like…

For about a day.

The challenge of playing the 80 year-old king was, of course, enormous. When I attempt the storm scene as part of *Lot o' Shakespeare*, I always come away both emotionally and physically drained. And then it hit me.

I still had a few years to go before my "Lear days" were behind me.

Hamlet, on the other hand?

Tick-tock.

The moment I decided to tackle *Hamlet*, I e-mailed my new Danish friend to tell him my plans.

"If anybody can do it, you can," he wrote back.

Oh, great. Now I have to justify him having that kind of faith in me.

But, of course, knowing that somebody had that belief in my ability drove me onward, wanting to see what it was that he might have seen in me, and just what all that had to do with *Hamlet*.

The first resource I revisited was the terrific Canadian series, *Slings & Arrows*, which features a Canadian Shakespeare Company producing *Hamlet* with a young movie star in the title role. The star is having a meltdown on opening night, unsure of himself, and the director (who had also played the role, and had his own breakdown in the process) asks:

"How are you on the soliloquies? You got those?"

"Yeah, I'm good on those… but there's all that stuff in between."

"Filler. You nail those six speeches, everybody goes home happy."

And so the soliloquies seemed to be the best place to start. If I was going to unpeel the onion that was this famously dense character, I really needed to know his inner thoughts. And the only place you can hear what's really happening inside Hamlet is *when he is speaking alone.*

I'd been working with the "Too, too solid flesh" speech for years. (A series of exercises around this takes up a long chapter in my acting textbook, ***Acting at the Speed of Life; Conquering Theatrical Style.***) I'd also memorized "To be or not to be" for ***Lot o' Shakespeare***, so I revisited those while adding "O, what a rogue and peasant slave am I," "Tis now the very witching time of night," "Now might I do it pat," and "How all occasions do inform against me."

I was beginning to find my footing within ***Hamlet***, and I was also adding my own sense of humanity, as well as my theatrical instinct to the mix. My Hamlet was no "melancholy Dane," feeling sorry for himself. Nor was he indecisive, save for that one moment when he cannot bring himself to kill the praying king. He *was ambivalent*, in the sense that the ambivalent person wants to take *all* possible paths, and as a result, ends up moving nowhere!

But to me, Hamlet is furiously in action, stage-managing the perfect takedown of the king who has stepped in to steal his father, his mother, his crown and his birthright. And it is, in fact, Hamlet's *reckless impulsiveness*, as he stabs Polonius "in the arras," that deals him his greatest setback.

With the soliloquies digested, I expanded the palate to include the major set speeches: "The king doth wake tonight and takes his rouse," "Angels and ministers of grace defend us," "And shall I couple hell?," "Speak the speech I pray you," "Oh, shame, where is thy blush?," "Alas, poor Yorick!," and "I am dead, Horatio. Wretched queen, adieu!"

And while I studied those, I was also studying some of my favorite sources. I turned, as always, to Isaac Asimov and his infinitely helpful *Asimov's Guide to Shakespeare,*[1] always the best source for understanding the historical, political and mythical background from which these plays emerge. (It's out of print; find a copy while you still can!)

---

[1] Asimov, Isaac, "Asimov's Guide to Shakespeare," 1978, Avenel Books; Reissue edition, New York.

I touched on Harold Bloom's *Shakespeare: The Invention of the Human*,[2] which (while somewhat hyperbolic), makes a great case for the supreme quality of this play. I also enjoyed Ron Rosenbaum's depiction of the many battles over Shakespearean text (and his takedown of Bloom) in *The Shakespeare Wars*.[3]

And, in the process, I started to notice things myself:

At every turn, Hamlet questions what it is to be human, comparing man to beasts, comparing people to characters, comparing man to the god(s), and comparing sanity to madness.

- What does it mean to be able to choose to remain alive, rather than existing simply by default?
- What does it mean to feel something deeply on the inside, even if that feeling does not manifest in action?
- What does it mean to take another's life?
- And to what end is "greatness" relevant if twenty years after one's death, all that is left is the skull itself?
- ...or if a man may eat of the fish that hath eaten of the worm that hath eaten of the king?
- ...or if Alexander, or Caesar, themselves, have long been reduced to loam whereof we might stop a beer barrel?

These themes dance back and forth in my head, and while they're busy dancing, I notice particular words.

Shakespeare, of course, had an unfathomable vocabulary, with 31,534 different words in his published works, drawn from a likely vocabulary of 66,000 words. He also *invented* some 1,700 or so words by himself!

So when **Hamlet** employs words multiple times in its text, words that I don't notice quite so often in Shakespeare's other plays, it sets off a little "ding" in my head, and I allow myself to consider that Shakespeare wants us to think about these concepts more particularly as they resonate through this particular play. Sometimes, it's like seeing a picture puzzle lying unassembled on a card table. We can see the colors, the textures, and we know immediately which pieces belong together, more or less.

[2] Bloom, Harold, "Shakespeare: the Invention of the Human," 1998, Riverhead Books, New York.

[3] Rosenbaum, Ron, "The Shakespeare Wars: Clashing Scholars, Public Fiascoes, Palace Coups," 2006, Random House, New York.

What follows here are words that are evocative of themes that Shakespeare seems to want us to be thinking about. And only the process of assembling the play, fitting those pieces together, will give us the whole picture (here, in mostly alphabetical order).[4]

Actions that a man might play
Their currents turn awry and lose the name of **action**
Suit the **action** to the word, the word to the **action**
Than I have **thoughts** to put them in, **imagination** to give them shape or time to **act** them in.
He keeps them, like an **ape**, in the corner of his jaw
To what **base** uses we may return, Horatio!
'Tis dangerous when the **baser nature** comes between the pass
Beast that wants discourse of reason
A **beast** no more
Now, whether it be **bestial** oblivion
Thus **conscience** does make **cowards** of us all
Is't not perfect **conscience**, to quit him with this arm?
And ever three parts **coward**
Am I a **coward**? Who calls me **villain**?
I am punish'd with sore **distraction**
There's a **divinity** that shapes our ends
A combination and a **form** indeed
His whole **function** suiting with **forms** to his conceit
Grace and **mercy** at your most need help you
See, what a **grace** was seated on this brow
Rightly to be **great**
One that would circumvent **God**, might it not?
His heels may kick at **heaven**
Words without thoughts, never to **heaven** go
They imitated **humanity** so abominably
Why may not **imagination** trace the noble dust of Alexander
As **pure** as grace, as **infinite** as man may undergo
How noble in reason! How **infinite** in **faculty**!
And waits upon the **judgment**: and what **judgment**…
Of accidental **judgments**, casual slaughters
Your noble son is **mad**
For **madness** would not err

---

[4] To capture every instance of some of these words would more than double the length of this sampling. Instead, I've simply plucked out those which shouted out to me for attention at any given moment, all drawn from this present "reckless slicing."

What is a **man?**
Exposing what is **mortal** and unsure
As if it were Cain's jaw-bone that did the first **murder!**
Here, thou **incestuous, murderous, damned** Dane
If thou hast **nature** in thee, bear it not
Had he the motive and the cue for **passion** that I have?
Tear a **passion** to tatters
And **reason** panders **will**
Sweep to my **revenge**
I am very **proud, revengeful, ambitious**
O, this is hire and salary, not **revenge**
Thoughts beyond the reaches of our **souls**
Could force his **soul** so to his own conceit
Been struck so to the **soul** that presently they have proclaimed their
malefactions.
Even with the very comment of thy **soul**
Let not ever the **soul** of Nero enter this firm bosom
To give them seals, never my **soul**, consent
Whose **spirit** with divine **ambition** puffed
The **treacherous** instrument is in thy hand
Let me be cruel, not **unnatural**
Of carnal, **bloody** and **unnatural** acts
One may smile, and smile and be a **villain**
That's **villainous** and shows a most pitiful **ambition**
Remorseless, **treacherous**, lecherous, kindless **villain**! O, **vengeance!**
A **villain** kills my father
To show **virtue** her own feature
Assume a **virtue**, if you have it not
Your **worm** is your only emperor for diet

I collect these words, somewhere in the middle of this process, with the first
three acts memorized and the latter two mostly assembled. I have already
begun to realize the power that is in these words when they are all put
together, and I sense that the special magic that brings them together is easily
lost when we try to read this play like a book, or when we try to play it like a
modern psychological inquiry, brooding with methodical pausing.

Mostly, I find myself getting lucky. The "big speeches" carry most of the plot
of the play, and I find that I have had to sacrifice remarkably little in
tightening this play down to a single hour. Those astonishingly familiar lines,
the ones that the English speaking universe finds itself quoting and reciting on
a daily basis, have floated to the top, and will "pop" again and again, for an
audience which will be startled to realize just how much of their cultural
heritage is tied up in this play!

And yet, certain exchanges just have to be set aside. Back-and-forth dialogue is difficult to capture in a one-man show without descending into self-parody. If wishing could make it so, I would have included more of Hamlet's "running rhetorical rings" around Polonius, his piercing take-downs of Rosencrantz and Guildenstern, and his heartbreaking attacks on Ophelia. (When I have the room, I try to note these in the pages running parallel to the dialogue.)

In reducing this material to a one-man, one-hour drama, I am hoping that what we lose in personnel, dialogue and *mass*, we may make up for in unity of vision and ease of access. The economy of scale that a one-man show provides enables this work to travel in ways that the fully mounted *Hamlet* never could, realizing this vision for a public that might never, otherwise see through the challenging words to the mountaintop that this play presents… if not in its fully-mounted glory, then perhaps somewhere, let us say, in the mind's eye.

My intention is to rip into this like the roaring, thrilling revenge drama that it kind-of is, and to leave you, the observer, to pick up the pieces of these themes and make sense of them for yourselves. All of this stuff is there, and with Shakespeare, there are very few accidents.

And neither, with Shakespeare, are there long brooding pauses, and time for you, or for any of Shakespeare's characters to contemplate. While, yes, one hour is well under *Hamlet's* intended playing time, I believe that four-hour productions of this play have missed Shakespeare's intended rhythm and tone entirely. When Shakespeare described *Romeo & Juliet* as "the two hours traffic of our stage," he wasn't kidding. He may have *rounded down*, somewhat, but these plays "gallop apace like fiery-footed steeds," and when we feel that overwhelming sense of *motion* that lives in them, they also *move* us in unanticipatable ways.

Hamlet thinks WHILE he speaks, and his speaking reflects his learning, and his learning is the action of this play. And even though such thought processes may seem to be passive, quiet and contemplative, this is a roaring struggle of one man ripping and writhing his way out of a trap all the while, setting mousetraps of his own for his great nemesis… all the while trying to put an impossible frame around this photograph of what-it-is-to-be-human that might somehow make sense of it all.

Finally, as I move beyond the play's text, into my portrayal, (and these discussions of my portrayal), I have to move from the broad realm of vast possibility to individual specific dramatic choices… choices with which you may or may not agree, and, if the latter, which may annoy you to no end as I expound upon them at length. You may prefer, for instance, to make more rugged, "manly" choices for your interpretation of Claudius.

That is, of course, the necessary evil of moving any play from text to production, and is not intended to restrict or judge choices that you might make regarding these characters.

Tim Mooney, 2015

Cast of Characters

(...at least the ones who get the chance to speak in this version)

Narrator

Hamlet

King Claudius

Queen Gertrude

Laertes

Polonius

The Ghost

Ophelia

The First Player

Horatio

Prince Fortinbras

Time: 1050-ish

Place: Denmark

TIMOTHY MOONEY

Production Notes

The performance text is on the right-hand side of the following pages.

Act and Scene headings are intended to be read aloud, and most *italicized* bridging narrative is also spoken. Elipses (…) are to indicate to the reader cuts of material that I have excised from Shakespeare's original (if only to help the reader know where to look in the process of fleshing out, or researching the text).

The rare use of [Brackets] indicates a stage direction **not** intended to be recited aloud, as they are actions self-evident from the performance.

In staging this piece,[5] we used only the slightest of props: A throne (always present but never used until the final line of the play), a center stage rug (absorbing some of the impact from kneeling or rolling on the floor), a skull for Yorick, always present stage left as an ominous presence, but not acknowledged until Act V), and a glass of water and hand towel to drink and dry off in our one moment of "breath," transitioning from Act III to Act IV.

Lighting was almost as simple, with various settings for day vs. night, and "specials" for the ghost, for the praying King Claudius, and Fortinbras' final line. Some of the "another room in the castle" scenes, particularly in Act IV, were created as isolated areas of lighting stage left and stage right.

As we will discuss at great length within, this Hamlet interacts readily and often with the audience, turning them into Ophelia, Gertrude, Claudius, Horatio and the public at large, of whom Hamlet is often conscious and aware.

This published text, in performance, usually took about 64 minutes to perform (allowing for laughs and crowd reactions). When the performance absolutely needed to come in under 60 minutes, further cuts were made to the first player's "Hecuba" speech, Hamlet's "Advice to the Players" speech, the Player King's "I do believe you think what now you speak" speech (cut entirely), Hamlet's several riffs on the skulls in the graveyard, as well as his subsequent discussion of "Alexander."

---

[5] World premiere: Clockwise Theatre, Waukegan, IL, May, 2015, Bob Sanders, Artistic Director.

Here's what you will quickly get used to:
Throughout my narration (the italicized stuff on the right-hand pages, opposite from these left-side, "deep background" pages), I'm going to give you information that Shakespeare generally doesn't state directly, but rather lets you come to realize over the course of a scene or scenes, learning by context.

As suggested by the title of this work, we don't have the time for that kind of "slow reveal" here. Thus, the quick exposition of Fortinbras' invasion: its relevance begins and ends this play, and needs to be known, though Shakespeare goes the long way around to bring us there.

And, yes, that's kind of the point with this script: I am "turning on the fire hose" of information, getting the glut of background out of the way fast so that we can absorb "the good stuff" fully, and in the moment that we need to.

*On one level, yes, it's fun to do it fast. But also, we modern observers, secure in our homes and the safety of our national borders might be slow to realize the emergency an Elizabethan audience would instantly perceive from the clues laced throughout this opening scene: **Danger is imminent and war is looming**. If you can grasp that in the 45 seconds that Act I, Scene 1 now takes, we can race on ahead with our attention still fully focused. (Jumping to Scene 2, without having performed ANY of the Scene 1 dialogue, always gets a laugh.)*

It's uncertain how good of a friend Horatio* is at the outset of the play. Hamlet calls him his "good friend" at their first encounter, but Horatio never seems so presumptive as to claim such close ties to the Prince.

As the play progresses, however, Horatio has clearly become Hamlet's only true, trusted friend, standing in stark contrast to those false friends, Rosencrantz and Guildenstern, as well as his nemesis and foil, "the angry Laertes."

---

* You may also notice that arrows are occasionally employed to explain which passage of the text a given discussion is intended to illuminate.

ACT I SCENE I: Elsinore. A platform before the castle.

The Norse prince, young Fortinbras, has been fighting to recapture territories in Denmark, and the Danish castle at Elsinore is nervously guarded around the clock by men who twice witness a strange apparition: A ghost! Seemingly in the guise of the late King Hamlet (whose son, young Hamlet, has recently returned from college at Wittenburg to attend his father's funeral).

The guards entreat Horatio (a friend of Hamlet's also back from Wittenburg), to witness and address the ghost who shows up for the third night in a row, almost on cue. Just as Horatio's urging seems to have coaxed the Ghost into speaking, signs of the approaching dawn drive it away.

More than Kin and less than Kind

Hamlet's "kin/kind" quip actually **follows** Claudius' Norway/Laertes snubs, but I find it crucial to drive the modern audience directly to the understanding that Hamlet has been cheated out of the kingship: the most oft-overlooked motivating force in this play.

The Elizabethan audience would have been acutely aware of the empire-shaking consequences a disruption of natural succession would bring about. Shakespeare wrote at least 10 plays dealing with such disturbances (the Histories), and for the audience of 1600, the ramifications of that history (the War of the Roses and the Hundred Years War) were every bit as present as our own Revolutionary War, Civil War and World War II are to us.

Claudius barely gets out "How is it that the clouds still hang on you?" before Queen Gertrude "piles on," forcing Claudius' to back her up with a more confrontational argument than he may have intended. This "tag-teaming" will echo in the very next scene as both Laertes and Polonius find fault with Ophelia.

Gertrude's petulant quibble springs from the awkward sense that Hamlet's "display" of grief is an overt indictment of her new marriage. Hamlet's somewhat smarmy reply ("Seems?") drives Claudius to come down harder than he'd perhaps intended. He can't have the young Prince openly criticizing the queen... nor can he have the shut-out heir to the throne as source of open and public rivalry. Thus, the announcement of Hamlet's succession lets a bit of steam out of that pressure cooker.

Is Hamlet bitter? Cynical? Sarcastic? Honestly grieving? When presented with such a choice, more often than not, I choose the path that **takes less time**, and bitter grief grinds the action to a crawl at this crucial outset of the play.

A heartsick Hamlet, honestly tearful over his father's loss, will take a much longer time to stumble through this defense of his emotional state. Whereas an angry Hamlet, jumping all over his mother for an inadvertent word choice, sets the action in motion forcefully. (Of course, some aspect of both emotional states can abide within Hamlet together.)

Hamlet's grief over these past two months may well be honest, but **it has been two months!** And mourning garb may well be Hamlet's only available way of openly declaring I AM NOT HAPPY WITH THE NEW KING!

I will have more to say about Claudius odd use of "unmanly grief" ahead...

Act I, SCENE II. A room of state in the castle.

Hamlet describes the way that King Claudius, his uncle (and, now, stepfather), treats him in court as, "A little more than kin and less than kind." *With the alteration of a single letter, Hamlet might also complain of being "less than king" as well.*

Claudius, in a power grab, quickly married the widow of the late King Hamlet, Queen Gertrude, thus setting himself up to take over as king. Holding court, he evades the brooding, envious glare of his nephew, Hamlet, arranging, instead, for a delegation to Norway to alert the uncle of young Fortinbras of his nephew's trespasses on Danish soil, and giving leave to Laertes, the son of his advisor, counselor and lackey, Polonius, to return to France.

Finally pivoting to his Nephew-slash-Stepson, Hamlet, Claudius begins to criticize Hamlet's sullen attitude, and Queen Gertrude quickly piles on, questioning why this display of grief seems so particular with him.

HAMLET
Seems, madam! nay it is; I know not 'seems.'
'Tis not alone my inky cloak, good mother,
Nor customary suits of solemn black,
Nor windy suspiration of forced breath,
No, nor the fruitful river in the eye,
Nor the dejected 'havior of the visage,
Together with all forms, moods, shapes of grief,
That can denote me truly: these indeed seem,
For they are actions that a man might play:
But I have that within which passeth show;
These but the trappings and the suits of woe.

Claudius continues to browbeat Hamlet for his "obstinant condolement," *and* "unmanly grief." *And yet, he proceeds to name Hamlet as successor to the throne, which can hardly be much consolation: had Hamlet gotten back to Elsinore before Claudius made his move, he might himself already be king. Alone, Hamlet ruminates:*

Too, too solid flesh...

This soliloquy gets an extended chapter in my acting textbook, "Acting at the Speed of Life; Conquering Theatrical Style." It is worth noting how fragmented the lines are: how many of his own sentences Hamlet interrupts with conflicting thoughts, and how many thoughts are left unfinished. This points to an internal turmoil within Hamlet that is rare for this era. Hamlet is one of the very few characters in literature that actually argues with himself (what Harold Bloom refers to as an aspect of Shakespeare's "invention of the human"). Rather than a single point of view pursued to its logical conclusion, Hamlet thrashes, trying to fight his way out of the intellectual box in which he has trapped himself.

Hamlet's soliloquy, describing the world as "stale, flat... an unweeded garden that grows to seed... rank and gross," anticipates the coming observation, that "something is rotten in the state of Denmark." Whatever happens in the subsequent acts of this play, this state of affairs can not be allowed to stand.

Hamlet's disgust with the world at large disguises a very particular issue with his mother and stepfather. This marriage followed "hard upon" his father's funeral, and while one cannot blame Hamlet for his sense of revulsion, his most prominent, repeated, obsessive concern is over the hurried rush of the wedding: "two months dead..." "within a month..." "a little month..." "to post with such dexterity..."

It was the **speed** of the wedding which kept Hamlet from his inheritance. Gertrude might have married any other man, but a match to the late King's brother, the one man near enough to the throne to assume it immediately, launched him into the kingship, while elbowing Hamlet out of his birthright. Of course, this also retained Gertrude the privileges of Queenship, rather than the empty role of "Queen Mother," so it was a win-win from her point of view.

This may be the most famous climax of a Shakespeare monologue: "To post with such dexterity to incestuous sheets!" is a tongue-twister fraught with emotion, imagery and struggle. The process of squeezing out those last two words at the tail end of a single breath can leave the actor spent, with tears in his eyes, and saliva spraying from the lips. It's a moment of emotional ugliness from which Hamlet must recover, with a final couplet of twenty single-syllable words (assuming that "cannot" counts as two separate words), sixteen of which end with a hard consonant: like a set of rusty brakes, bringing this impassioned soliloquy to a dead stop. (One-syllable words, especially those that end in a consonant, slow one's delivery of a given line.)

"Foul deeds will rise..." always reminds me of a seed germinating underground, unnoticed and unseen, until it springs rather quickly and evidently into view. In performance I tend to illustrate this visually, with one hand holding down the other fist, which pierces this barrier, opening out as the hand rises.

8

HAMLET

O, that this too too solid flesh would melt
Thaw and resolve itself into a dew!
Or that the Everlasting had not fix'd
His canon 'gainst self-slaughter! O God! God!
How weary, stale, flat and unprofitable,
Seem to me all the uses of this world!
Fie on't! ah fie! 'tis an unweeded garden,
That grows to seed; things rank and gross in nature
Possess it merely. That it should come to this!
But two months dead: nay, not so much, not two:
So excellent a king; that was, to this,
Hyperion to a satyr; so loving to my mother
That he might not beteem the winds of heaven
Visit her face too roughly. Heaven and earth!
Must I remember? why, she would hang on him,
As if increase of appetite had grown
By what it fed on: and yet, within a month--
Let me not think on't--Frailty, thy name is woman!--
A little month, or ere those shoes were old
With which she follow'd my poor father's body,
Like Niobe, all tears:--why she, even she--
O, God! a beast, that wants discourse of reason,
Would have mourn'd longer--married with my uncle,
My father's brother, but no more like my father
Than I to Hercules: within a month:
Ere yet the salt of most unrighteous tears
Had left the flushing in her galled eyes,
She married. O, most wicked speed, to post
With such dexterity to incestuous sheets!
It is not nor it cannot come to good:
But break, my heart; for I must hold my tongue.

Horatio tells Hamlet of the strange appearance of the ghost, and Hamlet
eagerly anticipates joining the watch that night

HAMLET

Till then sit still my soul; foul deeds will rise,
Though all the earth o'erwhelm them, to men's eyes.

The safety and health of his whole state

As Laertes describes the "political consideration" to which Hamlet is subject, he makes what may seem like an overstatement. But it serves us to keep in mind that "on his choice depends the safety and health of his whole state."

There was always great strategy in the selection of the wife of a prince or king. If Fortinbras had a sister, for instance, a wedding between her and Hamlet might have formed the base of an alliance between Denmark and Norway. That alliance might have kept tens of thousands of Danes safe from Norse invasion. Such couplings were often negotiated and decided while the proposed mates were still toddlers. And should the husband from such a marriage die, the widow would likely be snatched up immediately by a royal bachelor, a lord or a great land-owner, to expand the national holdings or to strengthen a treaty between two nations. Such negotiations were happening in the background throughout Shakespeare's History plays, though rarely mentioned. (It is worth noting just how much the fortunes of John of Gaunt and his son, Henry IV were improved by way of their talent for marrying well... and often.)

Following her husband's death, Gertrude became a great prize, and given that women were often disallowed from owning significant property in their own right, it made her desire to remarry quickly that much more urgent.

Beyond marriage, however, Hamlet's choices impact the entire state, and those choices decide not only his own life or death, but the vitality, peril and survival of every being in Norway. Whatever game Hamlet is playing here, he is playing it with tens of thousands of lives at stake, and it is the impact on those lives that give us the play's final resolution.

Quoting Shakespeare

Hamlet calls Polonius a "tedious old fool," and we have no reason not to agree. It makes it the more bewildering (to me, at least) to see some of these lines endlessly quoted as if they were divinely inspired, or (perhaps worse) as if they were Shakespeare's own deeply held sentiments. Isaac Asimov notes that "Neither a borrower nor a lender be" has become "literature's greatest gift to the small of heart... How many skinflints who know not one other verse in Shakespeare are letter-perfect in this, to use at the first sign of another's need!"

And while "to thine own self be true" may hold a deep kernel of wisdom, it comes out of the mouth of a lying, conniving, distrustful, ambitious "climber," who spies on his own children, risking their very reputations for the sake of his personal advantage or self-satisfaction. Quoting this with the single attribution of "Shakespeare" overlooks that, however sincerely this sentiment may be applied, or how inspiring it may sound, it comes, not from Shakespeare, but Shakespeare's creation: a blustering "tedious old fool" (who, most likely, is not "true to any man").

Act I, SCENE III. A room in Polonius' house.

Laertes makes ready to leave for France, advising his sister, Ophelia, to keep her distance from her seeming boyfriend, Prince Hamlet, and the "trifling of his favour." *For even if Hamlet does, indeed, love her, as successor to the throne, his choice of mate is subject to political consideration, and she must not open her* "chaste treasure" *to his* "unmaster'd importunity."

Before he can get away, Laertes' father, Polonius, cannot resist one last chance to load his son up with platitudes and advice, lecturing him with such tired bromides as, "Neither a borrower nor a lender be," *and* "To thine own self be true." *Once his son has left, Polonius redoubles Laertes' criticism of Ophelia, insisting that* "from this time forth [*she not*] give words or talk with the Lord Hamlet."

Invoking the Community: "Particular Men"

This speech is the first instance of several which will present themselves in which Hamlet (or, in one instance, Claudius) speak of the community. As such, it represents my first opportunity to engage the audience which is seated right there before me. When Hamlet speaks of "particular men," he has plenty at hand, only inches away, to regard and to comment upon. That fellow in the second row may be "nature's livery." The one off to the side may be "fortune's star." Others may be "pure as grace" or "as infinite as man may undergo..."

This enables us to grasp more completely a sense of individual characters that Hamlet may be envisioning, and to contemplate ourselves as part of some larger continuum, connected to Hamlet. It immediately drives the speech out of some sort of a generalized Elizabethan diatribe to a much more particular, present vision of this society which may well be "us."

Shakespeare, Moliere and their contemporaries were much more stylized and audience-interactive than we generally recognize. "Asides" are simply "the tip of the iceberg" of stylized behavior... a stylization so overt that it is impossible to play "realistically," and the editor cannot help but recognize it by adding that parenthetic "(Aside.)" in the printed text for clarification.

But like any iceberg, more than 90% of stylized behavior lies hidden from self-evident notice. This speech strikes me as our first good example of that behavior. There will be several instances more: When Hamlet sings the praises of mankind with "What a piece of work is man..." he will itemize a half dozen qualities of "man" easily represented by the surrounding audience.

In the midst of Hamlet's thunderous denunciation of Gertrude (which I already play to a select audience member, treating her as if she were the onstage "Gertrude"), Hamlet speaks of "flaming youth," and I find some younger woman in the audience (or a couple evidently out on a "date") to extend permission or forgiveness for their "compulsive ardor."

In Act IV, Claudius has his own soliloquy, exhorting "England" to kill Hamlet ("Do it, England!"). Although this is set in Denmark, when Claudius treats the present audience as if they were "England," we get a sense of the immediacy of Claudius conspiracy, and grasp the guilty horror the original audience might have felt from their own seeming complicity with the bad guy.

Each of these prepare us for Hamlet's final words, as he petitions : "You that look pale and tremble at this chance, That are but mutes or audience to this act..." Hamlet may be speaking metaphorically to the witnesses of the fencing match, but Shakespeare clearly has a feel for the sensation that ripples through the audience when a character recognizes them as co-conspirators in the drama. It propels this material into a presence of breathtaking immediacy.

Act I, SCENE IV. The platform.

Hamlet joins Horatio and the watchmen in their nightly vigil. In the distance, they hear trumpets and guns commemorating the king's revelry... which in Hamlet's depiction, sounds rather like a frat party.

HAMLET
The king doth wake to-night and takes his rouse,
Keeps wassail, and the swaggering up-spring reels;
And, as he drains his draughts of Rhenish down,
The kettle-drum and trumpet thus bray out
The triumph of his pledge.
... But to my mind, though I am native here
And to the manner born, it is a custom
More honour'd in the breach than the observance.
This heavy-headed revel east and west
Makes us traduced and tax'd of other nations:
They clepe us drunkards, and with swinish phrase
Soil our addition; and indeed it takes
From our achievements, though perform'd at height,
The pith and marrow of our attribute.
So, oft it chances in particular men,
...Carrying, I say, the stamp of one defect,
Being nature's livery, or fortune's star,--
Their virtues else--be they as pure as grace,
As infinite as man may undergo--
Shall in the general censure take corruption
From that particular fault...

The ghost arrives!

Angels and Ministers of Grace Defend Us!

This first line enjoys a second life outside of this play as the sometimes "antidote" to the famous "Macbeth Curse." Superstition has it that naming or quoting the play "Macbeth" (outside of rehearsal or performance) brings bad luck. And the only way to counter this is to engage in some cleansing ritual, such as spinning around three times and spitting, or speaking this line. (I parody this in my one-man play "Lot o' Shakespeare by forcing the audience to say "Angels and ministers of grace defend us!" each time I say "Macbeth.") And, after all, who wouldn't want "angels and ministers of grace" defending them?

It is only after much avoidance that Hamlet dares address the ghost as his father. An audience in a theatre will much more readily accept the return of the dead from the afterlife than someone actually confronted with a known dead parent. As he will later note, "The devil hath power to assume a pleasing shape," and it is crucial that Hamlet does NOT assume this ghost is his father, and must, therefore, not trust him outright. Only the play-within-the-play can prove the ghost's charges (while also gathering witnesses to Claudius' guilt).

Desperate for clues, Hamlet drags through a long prelude before even daring to attach the name "Hamlet" to this ghost. Getting no response, he tests his father's several preferred titles, and recounts the contradictory evidence of the funeral witnessed only days prior.

Still no response. Hamlet "pushes his luck," alluding to the ghost as "dead corse," noting that the corpse's presence has "made night hideous," which is, perhaps, not the most cordial welcome-home for one's lost father. (Hamlet softens this a bit by blaming the "thoughts beyond the reaches of our souls.")

At last Hamlet drives the point home with three unavoidable questions, and the ghost must respond. Left out of this sped-up version is the elaborate tangle between Hamlet, Horatio and the guards, who, fearing the ill intent of the ghost, do not want Hamlet to follow (or to follow alone), stirring Hamlet's response, "I'll make a ghost of him that lets [hinders] me."

Horatio's greatest fear is that the ghost may tempt Hamlet to suicide, an act that would taint Hamlet's "immortal soul." At almost every stage of this play, characters, weighing the dangers to their lives, are placing greater weight on how the nuances of these actions will impact their souls... thus further tangling each consideration of this play in the thicket of Catholicism.

Is it possible to overstate the relevance of "Something is rotten in the state of Denmark?" Despite the play's title, and the great dominance of the central character, we will ultimately discover that this play is every bit as much about Denmark as it is about "Hamlet," and only a full appreciation of this line will allow us to find the end of the play aesthetically and emotionally satisfying.

HAMLET

Angels and ministers of grace defend us!
Be thou a spirit of health or goblin damn'd,
Bring with thee airs from heaven or blasts from hell,
Be thy intents wicked or charitable,
Thou comest in such a questionable shape
That I will speak to thee: I'll call thee Hamlet,
King, father, royal Dane: O, answer me!
Let me not burst in ignorance; but tell
Why thy canonized bones, hearsed in death,
Have burst their cerements; why the sepulchre,
Wherein we saw thee quietly inurn'd,
Hath oped his ponderous and marble jaws,
To cast thee up again. What may this mean,
That thou, dead corse, again in complete steel
Revisit'st thus the glimpses of the moon,
Making night hideous; and we fools of nature
So horridly to shake our disposition
With thoughts beyond the reaches of our souls?
Say, why is this? wherefore? what should we do?

The Ghost beckons Hamlet to follow him away from the others, who are left intoning ominously, "Something is rotten in the state of Denmark."

"Responsive Man of Action..."

Of course, Hamlet is famous for quite the opposite... Yet I would argue that Hamlet is tagged unfairly with this. Our unfamiliarity with the political landscape Hamlet must negotiate makes it seem he is doing nothing through the great bulk of this play. Even Laurence Olivier (hilariously) misinterprets this in the opening titles to his 1948 film, which announce, "This is the tragedy of a man who could not make up his mind." (His subsequent performance proceeds to feature a lot of pausing and muttering under his breath...)

Here is an open question that Shakespeare never answers: When did Claudius' affair with Gertrude begin? To hear the Ghost tell it, it started before the assassination, which means that Gertrude was not the **victim** of Claudius scheming machinations... she was somehow **complicit** in creating the "rank and gross... nasty sty" that Denmark has become. Probably Gertrude was unaware of Claudius' intent to kill Hamlet-the-elder, but yet she must have at least noticed that his death sure was awfully convenient for Claudius... and she must have also realized that her hasty marriage had the impact of denying her son his birthright (while enabling her to remain Queen that much longer).

However old Hamlet is, just imagine spending over 20 years anticipating your impending coronation, only to have that pulled out from under you and put off for an unknown, uncertain period... perhaps as much as another 20 years! No wonder Hamlet is angry... and probably every bit as upset about this than about his father's actual death.

But back to the open question: How long before Hamlet's death did the affair begin? A week? A year? A decade? 30 years? It's not likely to have been that long, but Shakespeare **does not rule it out**... which leaves us, and Hamlet, with an unanswerable question: Who is Hamlet's father?*

And, on the wildly improbably chance that Claudius is Hamlet's father, what greater penalty might Heaven hold for a man who kills his own father than for one who kills his uncle?

The more "horrible" that the Ghost depicts the afterlife (a state which might have been avoided with a night of prayer, for all we know), the more necessary Hamlet will see it to dispense justice of equivalent severity.

It would be one thing for Hamlet to learn that Claudius had killed his father, but to hear it from his father, himself, and to learn of the punishment his father suffered following that swift dispatch, layers a secondary responsibility on Hamlet's shoulders: Claudius' death **and** punishment in the afterlife. It's a responsibility that should only, rightfully, belong to God, and Hamlet will be forced to overreach to achieve any semblance of justice.

* Credit to Harold Bloom ("Shakespeare, The Invention of the Human") for pointing this out.

Act I, SCENE V. Another part of the platform.

Hamlet catches up with the Ghost, who speaks at last, explaining that, given his "sudden and unnatural death," *there was no opportunity to seek forgiveness during life, and he is now doomed to burn off his sins amid the fires of purgatory. He reveals that his sudden death was not the result of a serpent sting, as had been given out, but rather a* "foul and most unnatural murder," *which his son must quickly avenge.*

Hamlet, famous, of course, as a swift, responsive man-of-action, insists:

HAMLET
Haste me to know't, that I, with wings as swift
As meditation or the thoughts of love,
May sweep to my revenge.

The Ghost reveals "The serpent that did sting thy father's life now wears his crown," *explaining how Claudius, won Queen Gertrude over to* "shameful lust," *and stole upon him while he slept in the garden, pouring a vial of poison into his ear.*

GHOST
…Thus was I, sleeping, by a brother's hand
Of life, of crown, of queen, at once dispatch'd:
Cut off even in the blossoms of my sin,
No reckoning made, but sent to my account
With all my imperfections on my head:
…O, horrible! O, horrible! most horrible!
If thou hast nature in thee, bear it not;
Let not the royal bed of Denmark be
A couch for luxury and damned incest.
… Adieu, adieu! Hamlet, remember me.

O Earth!

Most productions find Hamlet collapsing to the ground at this point. Through the course of his renewed encounter with Horatio and the Watchmen (on the following page), the Ghost, despite having exited, continues to shout "Swear" from offstage, or below the stage. (Not depicted in this version.)

The context of Hamlet's lines to the Ghost ("You hear this fellow in the cellerage" and "Can't thou work in the earth so fast?") suggest that the Ghost has returned to an underground habitat. As such, with "O earth," I let Hamlet go down to his hands and knees, thereby finding himself facing the "Hell" that he fears to "couple." This makes some sense of addressing his "sinews" which he then forces to "Bear me stiffly up."

There is something slightly comic about Hamlet's passionate insistence that he will wipe all thoughts from his brain, leaving only his father's commandment in place, and yet immediately leaves those thoughts behind to scorn his mother.

Hamlet, back from college, is apparently a prodigious note-taker. And some productions feature him producing a notepad (a "table" or "tablet") from somewhere on his person, to jot down this earth-shattering discovery: "That one may smile and smile and be a villain." While this makes a certain kind of sense of this passage, the question of what such a prop might have demanded, either in Shakespeare's day or in the year 1050, raises more questions than it satisfies, particularly how Hamlet, on an empty stage, might have a hard surface to write upon, and an inkwell to dip what we may assume would have been a quill. As such, I allow Hamlet to pantomime his planned essay on this great discovery (which he will assumedly compose as soon as he gets back to his room), while keeping his focus on the villain, Claudius, whom I envision sitting somewhere in the front row.

It may be so in Denmark

Again, we note that, while Claudius is a clear villain, the problem lies every bit as much with "Denmark": where murder and licentious incest, allowed to run free, and even to prosper... are rewarded with a throne. Since we never observed the process with which Claudius was anointed king, we are mostly immune to the back-room machinations, politics and arm-twisting that might have influenced this decision. But Shakespeare never lets go of the larger issue polluting the state of Demark at large, which is only exemplified by "The royal bed of Denmark [being] a couch for luxury and damned incest."

In fact, the most likely enabler of this corruption is the spying, "tedious old fool," Polonius, the only lord that we actually meet who would likely have been in on the nomination and confirmation of Claudius as king. Any hope for a actual, complete cleansing of Denmark would demand, not only the removal of Claudius, but Polonius as well.

HAMLET

O all you host of heaven! O earth! what else?
And shall I couple hell? O, fie! Hold, hold, my heart;
And you, my sinews, grow not instant old,
But bear me stiffly up. Remember thee!
…Yea, from the table of my memory
I'll wipe away all trivial fond records,
All saws of books, all forms, all pressures past,
…And thy commandment all alone shall live
Within the book and volume of my brain!
O most pernicious woman!
O villain, villain, smiling, damned villain!
My tables,--meet it is I set it down,
That one may smile, and smile, and be a villain;
At least I'm sure it may be so in Denmark:
So, uncle, there you are. Now to my word;
It is 'Adieu, adieu! remember me.'
I have sworn 't.

Horatio finally catches up to Hamlet, who will explain only…

Making Sense of a Confusing Monologue

This speech, as short as it is, proved extremely difficult to memorize, and it wasn't until I fully deconstructed it that the nature of Hamlet's intended statements came through, and the agitation of Hamlet's emotional state was revealed. I began by taking out the **"goose chase,"** dropping out those lines (lined through to the right)

> There are more things in heaven and earth, Horatio,
> Than are dreamt of in your philosophy. But come;
> Here, as before, never, so help you mercy,
> How strange or odd soe'er I bear myself,
> As I perchance hereafter shall think meet
> To put an antic disposition on,
> That you, at such times seeing me, never shall,
> ~~With arms encumber'd thus, or this headshake,~~
> ~~Or by pronouncing of some doubtful phrase,~~
> ~~As 'Well, well, we know,' or 'We could, an if we would,'~~
> ~~Or 'If we list to speak,' or 'There be, an if they might,'~~
> ~~Or such ambiguous giving out, to~~ note
> That you know aught of me: this not to do,
> So grace and mercy at your most need help you, Swear.

which seemed to lead us nowhere. There are actors out there who can make this entire monologue work, but I knew immediately it wouldn't fit into the hour long race through this play that I was taking on.

I then reworked all of the **"inverted constructions"** that seem to fill this speech into the more common ways we are used to hearing these phrasings:

"Here, as before, never" ➜ "Here, as never before"
"How strange or odd soe'er" ➜ "However strange or odd"
"As I perchance heareafter shall think" ➜ "As I hereafter may think"
"At such times seeing me" ➜ "Seeing me at such times"
"This not to do" ➜ "Do not do this"
"So grace and mercy at your most need" ➜ "May you have grace and mercy when you most need it"

Having done that, I then lined through what seemed to me to be more **extraneous words**, until a **through-line** began to emerge, the core of what Hamlet is trying to say. I was left with :

But come; however I bear myself, never note that you know aught of me: so help you, swear."

Boiled down to that clear statement, Hamlet's intent rises to the surface, and I can proceed to **add back in** all of those other complicated phrases without losing the thread of Hamlet's thought, which leaves us with the speech, as I am now performing it, on the opposite page.

And finally, I can then question exactly why Shakespeare puts me through this rigmarole in the first place! This level of complexity is not an accident nor some inherent sadism that Shakespeare holds toward actors... Why is Hamlet so twisted, confused and confusing? Oh, that's right! He just saw a ghost! The ghost of the father he's been mourning for the last two months. And so:

He's a little freaked out right now.

HAMLET
There are more things in heaven and earth, Horatio,
Than are dreamt of in your philosophy. But come;
Here, as before, never, so help you mercy,
How strange or odd soe'er I bear myself,
As I perchance hereafter shall think meet
To put an antic disposition on,
That you, at such times seeing me, never shall ...note
That you know aught of me: this not to do,
So grace and mercy at your most need help you, Swear.
... Let us go in together;
And still your fingers on your lips, I pray.
The time is out of joint: O cursed spite,
That ever I was born to set it right!

Continued from Opposite Page:
_It's a process that we actors should be able to apply to Shakespearean
passages again and again:_
> _1) Drop out the goose chase._
> _2) Rework the inverted constructions_
> _3) Line through the extraneous words._
> _4) Find the through line._
> _5) Add the complicated stuff back in._
> _6) Ask:_
> _Is there a live, emotional/psychological reason why this stuff was so
> complicated in the first place?_
> _7) And then:_ **Play that.**

Act II

We have no idea how long it has been since the end of Act I. We may assume it has been at least two weeks and perhaps as long as two months... long enough for Hamlet to establish his "madness," for Claudius to send off for Rosencrantz and Guildenstern, who then proceed to make the trip back to Elsinore, and long enough for the delegation to go away to Norway and return.

Polonius and the State of Denmark

Here we see the depth of Polonius' hypocrisy. His lectures to his son and daughter may have seemed pretentiously sanctimonious, but here he demonstrates that he is altogether content to damage his son's reputation solely for the sake of unearthing any secrets Laertes might be hiding. He instructs the spy to spread rumors of Laertes reputation for "drinking, fencing, swearing, quarreling, drabbing" (visiting prostitutes). In light of this, Polonius' advice of "to thine own self be true" now rings extremely hollow.

We are left to wonder about Hamlet's visit to Ophelia, coming to her with "his doublet all unbraced," and "with a look so piteous in purport as if he had been loosed out of hell." Was Hamlet, indeed, feeling tormented by her sudden absence from his companionship? Or was he exploiting her feelings (as well as his own) to further his deception?

More often than not, the movie versions of Hamlet cannot resist depicting this encounter, even as Ophelia's description continues in voiceover. Given that our only extended observed encounter between Ophelia and Hamlet features Hamlet berating and browbeating her, we feel instinctively needful of seeing our leading man showing some desire or tenderness to his intended.

Polonius demonstrates further lack of respect and sensitivity for Ophelia's feelings, exploiting potential political advantage by parading Hamlet's intimacies with her before the king. Previously, upon hearing of Hamlet's "tenders" of affection for Ophelia, Polonius' first assumption had been that Hamlet's intentions were to "beguile" her into giving up her chastity. (To be fair: this was not uncommon in men of great power... then and now.)

But here, Polonius sees a strategic opening: knowing that Claudius is urgently seeking the cause of Hamlet's "madness," there may be a political opportunity: with proof of Hamlet's love of Ophelia, Polonius might get Claudius and Gertrude to advocate for a match; Claudius would naturally want to diminish the public desire for Hamlet's ascension to the throne, and marriage to a woman of lower status would dull the political advantage of Hamlet becoming king. (Denmark would acquire no new territories from Hamlet marrying a "local girl," and Hamlet's political status would suffer a significant blow.) Of course, it would have the secondary impact of elevating Polonius' daughter to princess, and himself as an in-law to the royal family.

ACT II is mostly about "Acting and Spying!"

Time has passed! Hamlet seems to have convinced most everyone that he is under the grip of some sort of madness.

SCENE I. A room in POLONIUS' house.

Polonius sends a spy to France, to snoop around and dig up dirt about his son's behavior while away.

Ophelia reports a disturbing encounter with Hamlet, who burst in upon her, grasping her by the wrist and staring at her in a kind of creepy way. Convinced that this is "the very ecstasy of love," Polonius drags her off to see the king.

Foils

Shakespeare surrounds Hamlet with a series of "foils"... Similar characters who, in a similar situation, will act differently, thus setting the main character in perspective. We may notice that there are many characters of a similar age to Hamlet: Laertes, Fortnibras, Horatio and Rosencrantz & Guildenstern. Whereas Rosencrantz & Guildenstern allow themselves to be co-opted by the King, we cannot imagine Horatio being anything other than a true friend.

Fortinbras, likewise, the son of a late king whose throne has passed to an uncle, seems to have grown into an opportunistic conqueror, drifting around with an army, picking fights wherever he sees fit. Meanwhile, Laertes, brought up by a repressive, hypocritical father, turns into an angry hothead after his father's death, seemingly ready to fight anyone who challenges his family's reputation.

Polonius

Everyone describes Polonius as a long-winded pedant, and actors are instinctively tempted to race through "long-winded" lines, but this is one of the few speeches where I take lots of time. The longer Polonius keeps us waiting for any sort of substance, the funnier this is, and while several other characters see him as a dottering old fool, he seems quite enamored with his own wit.

Some productions present Polonius as an intelligent, scheming, sinister "power behind the throne"... I go a different direction, seeing the theatricality in two things: 1) Polonius speaks at great length to no actual purpose. 2) Polonius thinks that he is being extremely clever.

Hamlet, himself, calls Polonius a "tedious old fool" and a "wretched, rash, intruding fool." And while Shakespeare and Hamlet likely differ in certain opinions, I suspect that Hamlet is probably closer to Shakespeare's own sympathies than any other character he created, voicing Shakespeare's own opinions more often than not.

Of course, Polonius just wasted night, day and time in the process of pointing out how this topic would waste those very things.

This is what we call a circular definition, defining the thing by the thing itself, rendering the definition, thereby, useless.

Gertrude has interrupted Polonius, demanding "more matter with less art" and Polonius seems to be quite flattered she has called him out on this. The Queen has, after all, recognized his artistry," and saying "I swear I use no art at all," is pure false humility. ("What, this old thing? It was just hanging in the closet.") He then proceeds to flatter himself by wandering through every bit of wordplay that strikes him – mad/true, true/pity, pity/true – cause/effect, cause defect, effect/defective – making himself all the more irritating in the process.

ACT II, SCENE II. A room in the castle.

King Claudius welcomes two of Hamlet's childhood companions, Rosencrantz and Guildenstern, to Elsinore. Convinced that Hamlet is somehow "faking it," Claudius engages them to use their friendship to find out just why Hamlet has been acting so crazy and to report back.

The delegation returns from Norway! Success! The Norse King has smacked back his Nephew, young Fortinbras, who is now only seeking permission to cross over Denmark on his way to go pick a fight with Poland, instead.

Polonius arrives with the explanation to Hamlet's madness! But first! He must engage in an epic display of Polonial long-windedness, winding his way around the answer for as long as humanly possible before finally producing a letter that Hamlet has written to Ophelia.

POLONIUS
My liege, and madam, to expostulate
What majesty should be, what duty is,
Why day is day, night night, and time is time,
Were nothing but to waste night, day and time.
Therefore, since brevity is the soul of wit,
And tediousness the limbs and outward flourishes,
I will be brief: your noble son is mad:
Mad call I it; for, to define true madness,
What is't but to be nothing else but mad?
But let that go.
...Madam, I swear I use no art at all.
That he is mad, 'tis true: 'tis true 'tis pity;
And pity 'tis 'tis true: a foolish figure;
But farewell it, for I will use no art.
Mad let us grant him, then: and now remains
That we find out the cause of this effect,
Or rather say, the cause of this defect,
For this effect defective comes by cause:
Thus it remains, and the remainder thus. Perpend.
I have a daughter--have while she is mine--
Who, in her duty and obedience, mark,
Hath given me this: now gather, and surmise.
'Doubt thou the stars are fire;
Doubt that the sun doth move;
Doubt truth to be a liar;
But never doubt I love...

Love/Move

In performance, I let "love" take the sound of "move," pronouncing it "loov," though it is possible that it was "move" which was actually pronounced "muhv." And yet, the only way this actually "pays off" as a joke is when the second, rhyming word of a couplet has to be twisted to create the "strange-sounding" pronunciation. Either way, the point is: "words change over time."

I take issue with the argument for the "visual rhyme," which I contend was never really a thing. A "visual rhyme" is a contradiction in terms: rhymes only exist based on the way that they sound. But because people stumble across unrhyming words in Shakespeare that happen to be spelled similarly, they jump to the conclusion that spelling somehow "counted" in rhyme. This, of course, fails to account for vast shifts in pronunciation over time. More importantly, taking that extra moment to "visualize" the rhyme can only take the audience out of the moment, distracting them from the live action.

Hamlet gets the better of Polonius. His play on "conception" (the generation of thought) vs. how Polonius' "daughter may conceive" (getting pregnant) pays off with Polonius' clueless observation of "how pregnant his replies are."

Hamlet and Rosencrantz & Guildenstern

I couldn't fit in Polonius' famous observation "Though this be madness, yet there is method in't," but it's worth considering that Hamlet's "madness" manifests differently with each person he encounters. While he leads Polonius in dizzying circles, he is more sincere with Rosencrantz & Guildenstern. His challenge is to maintain this seeming "insanity" without offending two men he still assumes to be friends. His essential explanation is, "see, everybody thinks that I'm crazy, but I'm really just depressed."

Even in the process of describing man as a "quintessence of dust," a bleak allusion to the disintegrating corpse that Hamlet will ultimately contemplate in Act V, he cannot get there without first leading us through one of the most glorious literary depictions of humanity ("What a piece of work is a man?").

Polonius is often depicted reading these lines from a flyer: after all, it sounds almost like an advertisement straight from the touring company itself. But that choice leaves the actor with very little investment in his dialogue. Polonius thinks himself a great wit, and a great judge of wit in others. And borrowing someone else's words off of a piece of paper does little to express that. I find it particularly hilarious if Polonius is improvising, repeatedly struck by yet another genre in which this troupe excels, and then realizing the sub-genres, all the way down to the absurd level of a four-pronged sub-genre that encompasses them all. I suspect that Shakespeare, himself, is having a laugh over the critic's need to pigeonhole a given work of theatre, preferring his own free-wheeling ability to express his muse in any given play as it suits him.

(This was from back in the day when "love" and "move" somehow seemed to rhyme.)

Polonius explains that it was his restriction of Hamlet's access to Ophelia which led him to "fall into the madness wherein he now raves, and we all mourn." *His solution: More spying! Polonius will use Ophelia as bait,* "loosening her to Hamlet" *while he and Claudius hide behind the tapestry (better known as "the arras") to* "mark the encounter."

Hamlet appears, and we wonder whether he might have overheard Polonius' plans to exploit his daughter. We see him enacting the role of "Mad Hamlet" for the first time, running rhetorical rings around Polonius...

HAMLET
Have you a daughter? ...Let her not walk i' the sun: conception is a blessing: but not as your daughter may conceive. Friend, look to 't.

Polonius is startled to note just "how pregnant sometimes his replies are."

Approached by Rosencrantz and Guildenstern, Hamlet grows suspicious as their inquiries grow more pointed, and after much prodding, finally gets them to admit they were, indeed, sent for by the king.

HAMLET
I will tell you why; so shall my anticipation prevent your discovery, and your secrecy to the king and queen moult no feather. I have of late—but wherefore I know not--lost all my mirth, forgone all custom of exercises; and indeed it goes so heavily with my disposition that this goodly frame, the earth, seems to me a sterile promontory, this most excellent canopy, the air, look you, this brave o'erhanging firmament, this majestical roof fretted with golden fire, why, it appears no other thing to me than a foul and pestilent congregation of vapours. What a piece of work is a man! how noble in reason! how infinite in faculty! in form and moving how express and admirable! in action how like an angel! in apprehension how like a god! the beauty of the world! the paragon of animals! And yet, to me, what is this quintessence of dust? man delights not me: no, nor woman neither, though by your smiling you seem to say so.

Polonius announces the arrival of:

POLONIUS
The best actors in the world, either for tragedy, comedy, history, pastoral, pastoral-comical, historical-pastoral, tragical-historical, tragical-comical-historical-pastoral, scene individable, or poem unlimited: Seneca cannot be too heavy, nor Plautus too light. For the law of writ and the liberty, these are the only men.

Shakespeare on Playwriting

This is a terrific insight to what Shakespeare, himself, may have thought of as keys to good playwriting. To him, "an excellent play" would feature "well digested" scenes that are "set down with as much modesty as cunning." By "well digested," we may assume that the author has taken sufficient time in their development, but the issue of "modest" vs. "cunning" strikes me as revelatory of Shakespeare's own style: As powerful as his work was, Shakespeare was not an especially flashy, or bombastic, writer, as were some of his contemporaries, such as Christopher Marlowe or Thomas Kyd.

In other words, though Shakespeare does draw his scenes with a certain degree of "cunning," that "cunning" is disguised behind a veil of "modesty," as Shakespeare puts the action of the play into the forefront of the audience' awareness over and above the personality of the writer... which may account for Shakespeare's own personality remaining so mysterious, deeply buried within the depths of "well digested" scenes.

What an amazing memory this actor must have! Assuming that this speech was never acted above once, and that Hamlet heard it some years before, the player's ability to perform it on demand seems almost superhuman... unless it is one of those independent performance pieces that an actor may do in auditions, or in a cabaret setting, or just between friends. Or, Shakespeare may be suggesting a level of craft that we tend to associate with master violinists or world-class pianists who maintain a vast repertory in performance readiness. This stands in effective contrast with Polonius' superficial dilettantism.

In "breaknecking" this scene, I cut past a false start, and a passage that Polonius complains of going on too long. Hamlet, disdaining Polonius as an aesthetic Philistine, only **then** proceeds to ask the First Player to jump on ahead to the tale of Hecuba.

A little time spent surfing the words "Aneas," "Dido," "Priam," "Hecuba" or "the sack of Troy," exploring even the slightest background on these ancient characters will greatly inform the understanding and delivery of this speech.

The challenge is to deliver this speech powerfully, with a full voice and style appropriate to a barnstorming troupe of the era, while still touching something real and human within. It helps to visualize the terror of the night the player has depicted: a ravaged city, an entirely humbled, vulnerable queen watching the heartless slaughter of her husband by a ransacking, marauding force.

This is one of Shakespeare's several great uses of the word "clamour." He seems to never use this word inadvertently, and here, amid these final lines, I believe is the real impassioned climax of this speech, an emotional breakdown that is necessary for Hamlet's next soliloquy to make any sense.

Hamlet welcomes the actors and, perhaps, testing out an idea, asks the leading player...

HAMLET
I heard thee speak me a speech once, but it was never acted; or, if it was, not above once... an excellent play, well digested in the scenes, set down with as much modesty as cunning... One speech in it I chiefly loved: 'twas Aeneas' tale to Dido; and thereabout of it especially, where he speaks of Priam's slaughter: if it live in your memory... Prithee, say on:... come to Hecuba.

First Player
'But who, O, who had seen the mobled queen--'
'Run barefoot up and down, threatening the flames
With bisson rheum; a clout upon that head
Where late the diadem stood, and for a robe,
About her lank and all o'er-teemed loins,
A blanket, in the alarm of fear caught up;
Who this had seen, with tongue in venom steep'd,
'Gainst Fortune's state would treason have pronounced:
But if the gods themselves did see her then
When she saw Pyrrhus make malicious sport
In mincing with his sword her husband's limbs,
The instant burst of clamour that she made,
Unless things mortal move them not at all,
Would have made milch the burning eyes of heaven,
And passion in the gods.'

A favorite exchange (that could not quite fit in this presentation): Hamlet asks Polonius to "see the players well bestowed." Polonius counters that he will "use them according to their desert." Hamlet replies: "Use every man after his desert, and who should scape whipping? Use them after your own honour and dignity: the less they deserve, the more merit is in your bounty."

Another example of the discipline expected of actors at this time: Hamlet will provide the First Player with an extra 12-16 lines to memorize within 24 hours, and the First Player is confident he will make those, yet unknown, lines work.

There is a modern joke, in which we say something seemingly sincerely, and then, pausing, tack on a sarcastic "not" almost as an afterthought. I like to think of "mock him... not" as being the forerunner of that practice.

Acting and Time

The acting pyrotechnics that have so astonished Hamlet here continue to impress audiences today. Even if we find ourselves 400 years removed from Hamlet, while Hamlet, in turn, predated the Elizabethan era by 450 years, the composition of The Iliad takes us back even further: another 1,800 years, while the Trojan War itself, reaches back another 500 years prior to that!

The farther removed a given act is in time, the more likely it is that we may dissociate ourselves from any attachment to the living passions that those characters felt, and Hamlet's astonishment about this artist of his own age parallels our own amazement over the contemporary actor's ability to identify with Hamlet, and reminds us that while the circumstances may shift, human nature and it's depiction remain timeless.

Since Shakespeare rarely does anything accidental, I cannot help but assume that Hamlet's listing of the King's "property" before his "most dear life" must reflect his priority. Yes, he is disturbed at the loss of his father's life, but what truly drives him is his own self-interest: the denial of "property" which should, by rights, be Hamlet's by now. As king, Hamlet would have been in control of vast wealth, property and power. Once Claudius "cuts in line," Hamlet can only "eat the air, promise-crammed" (a line from Act III).

"Property" may be a turning point for Hamlet. He shifts from brooding and melancholy into action, or, at the very least, goading himself into action. Hamlet has, so far, shown great restraint. The first soliloquy ("too, too solid flesh") is full of fits and starts as Hamlet interrupts himself repeatedly, and never quite hits the stride of a "rant" (though "to post with such dexterity to incestuous sheets" does flash with rage). But here, struck with the loss of father and "property," his bitterness gathers momentum, building to the extremes of "Oh, vengeance!..." (And Hamlet, once again struck with an ironic burst of self-awareness, climbs back down.)

As Polonius shows the players to their lodgings, Hamlet draws the lead actor aside...

HAMLET

Dost thou hear me, old friend; can you play the Murder of Gonzago? ... We'll ha't to-morrow night. You could, for a need, study a speech of some dozen or sixteen lines, which I would set down and insert in't, could you not?... Very well. Follow that lord; and look you mock him not.
...Now I am alone.
O, what a rogue and peasant slave am I!
Is it not monstrous that this player here,
But in a fiction, in a dream of passion,
Could force his soul so to his own conceit
That from her working all his visage wann'd,
Tears in his eyes, distraction in's aspect,
A broken voice, and his whole function suiting
With forms to his conceit? and all for nothing!
For Hecuba!
What's Hecuba to him, or he to Hecuba,
That he should weep for her? What would he do,
Had he the motive and the cue for passion
That I have? He would drown the stage with tears
And cleave the general ear with horrid speech,
Make mad the guilty and appal the free,
Confound the ignorant, and amaze indeed
The very faculties of eyes and ears. Yet I,
A dull and muddy-mettled rascal, peak,
Like John-a-dreams, unpregnant of my cause,
And can say nothing; no, not for a king,
Upon whose property and most dear life
A damn'd defeat was made. Am I a coward?
Who calls me villain? breaks my pate across?
Plucks off my beard, and blows it in my face?
Tweaks me by the nose? gives me the lie i' the throat,
As deep as to the lungs? who does me this?
Ha!
'Swounds, I should take it: for it cannot be
But I am pigeon-liver'd and lack gall
To make oppression bitter, or ere this
I should have fatted all the region kites
With this slave's offal: bloody, bawdy villain!
Remorseless, treacherous, lecherous, kindless villain!
O, vengeance!

What an ass am I!

Hamlet cannot help but laugh at himself. Perhaps he notices himself raging demonstratively, with his fists in the air... Perhaps his lips are wet with the inevitable spittle that "treacherous, lecherous" sprays out from him.

Here is another moment in which Hamlet, alone on stage, cannot help referencing the audience in front of him. He is, after all, staring straight into the faces of "guilty creatures, sitting in a play." To pretend that they are **not** there would be to ignore the great transformative question that this speech raises in the minds of the audience... "Am I a guilty creature?" "Might something in **this** play trip **me** up?" "Have I traveled backward in time, or has Shakespeare somehow reached forward to me?"

The odd question that this speech raises is: didn't Hamlet make this decision five minutes before, when he asked the First Player to play "The Murder of Gonzago?" Perhaps Hamlet had a vague sense of the appropriateness of the play, but has only now strategized his way through a plan. Or, perhaps his anger at himself has stirred his resolve to actually put this plan into action. Or, perhaps just as likely, the sudden awareness of the audience has brought him around to letting them in on the secret.

On the word of a Ghost

As Asimov points out, we hold different assumptions about ghosts in the modern world (assumptions which may well be the product of having seen these "visitation" scenes so often in drama). While today we might instantly assume that the ghost of our father is, indeed, our dead father, returned for a visit, for Hamlet, that ghost may well be a manifestation of a wicked spirit who only wants to trick him into damnation by killing a man without righteous reason. To proceed solely on the word of a ghost, who "may be the devil," might doom his soul to hell. And the anticipated afterlife is a very palpable thing in this play.

Indeed, he must first test the story of the ghost to see if it holds water. Hamlet is **not** indecisive. He is actively chasing down proof. And it turns out that quite a bit of this play's resolution rests on the question of what it means to die a good death... a death untainted by violation of the commandments. After all, assuming that the ghost was telling the truth, Hamlet already knows of the torture his father is now enduring, having died amid "the blossoms of his sin."

HAMLET *(Continued.)*
Why, what an ass am I! This is most brave,
That I, the son of a dear father murder'd,
Prompted to my revenge by heaven and hell,
Must, like a whore, unpack my heart with words,
And fall a-cursing, like a very drab,
A scullion!
Fie upon't! foh! About, my brain! I have heard
That guilty creatures sitting at a play
Have by the very cunning of the scene
Been struck so to the soul that presently
They have proclaim'd their malefactions;
For murder, though it have no tongue, will speak
With most miraculous organ. I'll have these players
Play something like the murder of my father
Before mine uncle: I'll observe his looks;
I'll tent him to the quick: if he but blench,
I know my course. The spirit that I have seen
May be the devil: and the devil hath power
To assume a pleasing shape; yea, and perhaps
Out of my weakness and my melancholy,
As he is very potent with such spirits,
Abuses me to damn me: I'll have grounds
More relative than this: the play 's the thing
Wherein I'll catch the conscience of the king.

"The Mt. Everest of Soliloquies"

"To be..." may well be our most challenging soliloquy, in no small part because of its **fame** as perhaps our most profound speech. Most actors struggle to "**feel**" the monologue as deeply as possible, often leading to pauses, sighs, and whispering. We have a vague sense that Hamlet may be contemplating suicide, but very little sense of his progress toward or away from that choice.

The way we always hear this opening line ignores the "scansion" of iambic pentameter. While everyone in the audience has braced themselves to hear:
>   "to **BE** or **NOT** to be; **THAT** is the **QUEST**ion,"
...the line actually "scans" as
>   "to **BE** or **NOT** to **BE**; that **IS** the **QUEST**ion."

When the speech begins this way, it feels like hearing a rock n' roll "standard" performed acoustically: the audience, startled into listening in a whole new way, hears words they never knew were in the lyrics. This time, it is a monologue about "being." And, in fact, this speech only touches on suicide (on "'tis a consummation devoutly to be wish'd"), dwelling more on taking a chance and putting life at great risk: "To take arms against a sea of troubles."

To die: to sleep; no more

It wasn't until I committed these six words to memory that I could finally make sense of this monologue. One can make an argument for at least three very different interpretations of these six words, but only one interpretation makes sense out of the rest of the monologue: "**To die**" is "**no more**" than "**to sleep!**"

"Perchance to dream" is a joyful vision of death, and here I turn the point of his blade (drawn at "take arms") toward my chest, ready to plunge it within until "dream" brings me up short, as Hamlet has no idea what a dead man's dreams may be. This, coincidentally finds me "rubbing" the spot on my chest where the blade pressed (on "there's the rub"). ("The rub" actually alludes to an obstacle in lawn bowling which takes the ball off of its intended path.")

It is the fear ("the respect") of those dreams that leads a man to drag life out, struggling (with "the calamity") to extend his life at all costs, and Hamlet enumerates that calamity: a list of eight "whips and scorns," some from the perpetrator: "The oppressor's wrong," "the proud man's contumley," "the insolence of office" – And some experienced by the victim: "the pangs," "the spurns that patient merit of the unworthy takes." And the actor may choose to see himself "delivering" or "enduring" this calamity, variously, which lends definition to what might otherwise play as a meaningless "list."

It is that last line that is Hamlet's most immediate and bitter pill to swallow. He, himself, has been patiently meritorious, accepting the "spurns of the unworthy," and the "unworthy," in Hamlet's mind, can only mean Claudius.

ACT III features even more acting and spying!

SCENE I. A room in the castle.
Happy to hear of any spark of inclination from Hamlet, Claudius readily agrees to attend the play that night. Meanwhile, Polonius sets the scene for Hamlet to encounter Ophelia, reading idly from a book. He and Claudius scurry off to hide behind the arras as Hamlet approaches.

HAMLET
To be, or not to be: that is the question:
Whether 'tis nobler in the mind to suffer
The slings and arrows of outrageous fortune,
Or to take arms against a sea of troubles,
And by opposing end them? To die: to sleep;
No more; and by a sleep to say we end
The heart-ache and the thousand natural shocks
That flesh is heir to, 'tis a consummation
Devoutly to be wish'd. To die, to sleep;
To sleep: perchance to dream: ay, there's the rub;
For in that sleep of death what dreams may come
When we have shuffled off this mortal coil,
Must give us pause: there's the respect
That makes calamity of so long life;
For who would bear the whips and scorns of time,
The oppressor's wrong, the proud man's contumely,
The pangs of despised love, the law's delay,
The insolence of office and the spurns
That patient merit of the unworthy takes,
When he himself might his quietus make
With a bare bodkin? who would fardels bear,
To grunt and sweat under a weary life,
But that the dread of something after death,
The undiscover'd country from whose bourn
No traveller returns, puzzles the will
And makes us rather bear those ills we have
Than fly to others that we know not of?

Having drawn Hamlet's sword or dagger, in pantomime, early on, holding it to my chest on "to sleep: perchance to dream," I also hold it to my throat on "his quietus make with a bare bodkin," and with the line, "their currents turn awry," return the blade to its sheath, slamming it angrily in place with "and lose the name of action."

More Acting and Spying

Some have suggested that Hamlet may be aware of Claudius and Polonius throughout this soliloquy. My instinct suggests that "To be" is already a heady challenge for the audience. Adding extra layers of insincerity (with Hamlet essentially **performing** the speech to confuse the spies), is more likely to confuse **us**. But, if this realization doesn't come until Hamlet has been cued by Ophelia's behavior, it helps explain his wild emotional swings. His anger stems from having realized, after the fact, that Claudius and Polonius have witnessed him being sincere and sane, and that Ophelia has colluded in that plot.

"Revengeful" and "ambitious" seem to be direct attacks at Claudius, upon whom he means to take revenge, and toward whose kingship he has ambition. Likewise, when Hamlet asks, "Where's your father?" Hamlet almost certainly knows Polonius is listening, and will thereby hear himself being called a fool.

Monsters

The term "monster" has come to suggest, almost exclusively, a being with evil super-powers. But the classic definition of a monster focuses more on a being that mixes traits of both man and beast, like a centaur or a vampire.

In the middle ages, a man who's wife had taken another lover would be derided as a "cuckold," a term drawn from the "cuckoo" (a bird which would lay eggs in another's nest), but which became identified more actively with the stag which would relinquish its mate when defeated by another male. Thus, a cuckolded man came to be identified as bearing the horns of a stag, and I perform the "cuckold gesture" on this word, placing my knuckle to my forehead with two fingers extended forward, symbolizing the horns that a cuckolded man supposedly grows (making him a "monster" of sorts).

Of course the "one" marriage which will not be allowed to "live," is that between Claudius and Gertrude, and, given Claudius' quick resolve to get rid of Hamlet, we may assume that Claudius interprets this as a direct death threat.

Having realized that he was overheard in an unguarded moment of sincerity, Hamlet veers wildly into his pretend-insanity, perhaps too sharply to convince Claudius that this sudden transformation is anything but an act. Unfortunately, Ophelia, bearing the full brunt of Hamlet's anger, has no such perspective, and finds herself caught "between the pass and fell incensed points of mighty opposites." (Act V, Scene 2.)

Thus conscience does make cowards of us all;
And thus the native hue of resolution
Is sicklied o'er with the pale cast of thought,
And enterprises of great pitch and moment
With this regard their currents turn awry,
And lose the name of action. – Soft you now!
The fair Ophelia! Nymph, in thy orisons
Be all my sins remembered.

When Ophelia attempts to return certain gifts that Hamlet has given her (in light of their seeming breakup), Hamlet immediately recognizes the insincerity in what is clearly a staged and (probably) an observed performance.

HAMLET
Ha, ha! Are you honest?... Are you fair?... If you be honest and fair, your honesty should admit no discourse to your beauty. ... for the power of beauty will sooner transform honesty from what it is to a bawd than the force of honesty can translate beauty into his likeness: this was sometime a paradox, but now the time gives it proof. I did love you once. ...You should not have believed me: I loved you not. ...Get thee to a nunnery: why wouldst thou be a breeder of sinners? I am myself indifferent honest; but yet I could accuse me of such things that it were better my mother had not borne me: I am very proud, revengeful, ambitious, with more offences at my beck than I have thoughts to put them in, imagination to give them shape, or time to act them in... Where's your father? ...Let the doors be shut upon him, that he may play the fool no where but in's own house. ...If thou dost marry, I'll give thee this plague for thy dowry: be thou as chaste as ice, as pure as snow, thou shalt not escape calumny. Get thee to a nunnery, go: farewell. Or, if thou wilt needs marry, marry a fool; for wise men know well enough what monsters you make of them. ...I have heard of your paintings too, well enough; God has given you one face, and you make yourselves another... Go to, I'll no more on't; it hath made me mad. I say, we will have no more marriages: those that are married already, all but one, shall live; the rest shall keep as they are. To a nunnery, go.

Ophelia is devastated. Claudius, now convinced that Hamlet is NOT mad, makes plans to get him out of Denmark as quickly as possible, shipping him off to England with Rosencrantz and Guildenstern.

Shakespeare on Acting

It is important to keep in mind the outrageous, bombastic, overblown style of performance popular at the time, that Shakespeare (via Hamlet) was railing against. Hamlet decries the typical portrayals of hideous villains (such as Termagant and Herod) who were probably portrayed as shrieking lunatics.

While we easily remember the lesson of the first lines of this speech, many acting teachers forget or ignore "Be not too tame neither." Hamlet argues not for subtlety in place of style, but for **appropriateness of action**, which demands a greater sensitivity to the only tool that Shakespeare was able to leave behind for our use: the words he intended for the actors to speak aloud. Shakespeare still wants his big moments to "rock the house," but they can only be truly effective if the actor emphasizes them as the moment, and the text, demand.

Sometimes Shakespeare puts a lot of meaning into a seemingly insignificant word: There is a special demand on the word "from" in this particular instance. Hamlet is suggesting that overacting works against, or **"at cross purposes"** with the very reason that they are putting on the play in the first place. As such, the actor needs to invest "from" with a special energy.

As Hamlet, I point my pantomimed mirror at the actors for "mirror up to nature," pivot it towards an imaginary virtuous person (Ophelia?) for "virtue her own feature," towards myself on "scorn her own image" and, most importantly, towards the throne on "the very age and body of the time..." In other words, the actors are responsible to reflect the king (who **is** "the age and body of the time") back to himself so that he might see his own "form and pressure." Since few might dare actually speaking "truth to power" only the theatre can provide the king with a perspective on the challenges he faces. This was a major virtue of the theatre: to reflect back to great lords their proper position when there is otherwise no "peer" from whom they might learn.

"Not to speak it profanely" may be very confusing, until we consider that "nature's journeymen" refers to the animal kingdom: in other words, the actors that Hamlet is describing acted as if they were the products of some bestial coupling (which is the "profane" act that Hamlet will not describe).

Hamlet, frozen out from arguing publicly against the evil of his uncle, somehow manages to vent his spleen vigorously when it comes to railing against comic actors who work the audience for laughs while disrespecting the dramatic narrative. In performance, I have my Hamlet caught up in such a fever over this that he inadvertently "saws the air with his hand" on "that's villainous, and shows most pitiful ambition..." He then catches himself waving his hand, which has effectively undermined his argument about acting, while also, perhaps, revealing the anger Hamlet has been suppressing. He has displaced bottled-up anger towards Claudius into an area where it is safe: aesthetic criticism!

38

ACT III, SCENE II. A hall in the castle.

In order for his plan to work Hamlet needs the players to be compellingly believable.

HAMLET
Speak the speech, I pray you, as I pronounced it to you, trippingly on the tongue: but if you mouth it, as many of your players do, I had as lief the town-crier spoke my lines. Nor do not saw the air too much with your hand, thus, but use all gently; for in the very torrent, tempest, and, as I may say, the whirlwind of passion, you must acquire and beget a temperance that may give it smoothness. O, it offends me to the soul to hear a robustious periwig-pated fellow tear a passion to tatters, to very rags, to split the ears of the groundlings, who for the most part are capable of nothing but inexplicable dumbshows and noise: I would have such a fellow whipped for o'erdoing Termagant; it out-herods Herod: pray you, avoid it. ...Be not too tame neither, but let your own discretion be your tutor: suit the action to the word, the word to the action; with this special observance: that you o'erstep not the modesty of nature: for any thing so overdone is from the purpose of playing, whose end, both at the first and now, was and is, to hold, as 'twere, the mirror up to nature; to show virtue her own feature, scorn her own image, and the very age and body of the time his form and pressure. Now this overdone, or come tardy off, though it make the unskillful laugh, cannot but make the judicious grieve; the censure of the which one must in your allowance o'erweigh a whole theatre of others. O, there be players that I have seen play, and heard others praise, and that highly, not to speak it profanely, that, neither having the accent of Christians nor the gait of Christian, pagan, nor man, have so strutted and bellowed that I have thought some of nature's journeymen had made men and not made them well, they imitated humanity so abominably. ...O, reform it altogether. And let those that play your clowns speak no more than is set down for them; for there be of them that will themselves laugh, to set on some quantity of barren spectators to laugh too; though, in the mean time, some necessary question of the play be then to be considered: that's villanous, and shows a most pitiful ambition in the fool that uses it. Go, make you ready.

BFF's: Horatio & Hamlet

Horatio's position as "Hamlet's best friend" solidifies through the play over a limited number of scenes. Through this conversation we learn that, following Act I, Scene 5, Hamlet has described his encounter with the ghost to Horatio, as he here alludes to "the circumstance which I have told thee of my father's death." This launches Horatio into the trusted position of the "keeper of the story," a story which will not die with Hamlet. It contrasts effectively with Rosencrantz and Guildenstern, who are seeking to parley their friendship with Hamlet into greater privilege. Having Horatio as confidante also keeps a real-world check on Hamlet, who cannot be sure he was not hypnotized or misled by the ghost.

In this scene, as with the speech to the players, I "localize" the imagined throne in space (usually elevated stage right) on "before the king" and "observe mine uncle." Once the audience is clear on where Claudius is seated, Hamlet's sudden raging look in that direction on "gets the love of Gonzago's wife!" is all we need to see the sharp accusation hitting Claudius like a baseball bat.

To the modern ear, the archaic "thee" and "thou" sound formal, but during Shakespeare's time, this was often indicative of a more intimate connection. Hamlet's use of it here reflects a more sincere, honest and perhaps, vulnerable relationship to Horatio, as he alludes to his most carefully protected secret. We may very well track who is "trending upwards" with Hamlet by his choice of language. (Hamlet bestows a single "thou" upon meeting R&G, but, discovering their newly-formed allegiance with the king, reverts to "you" from then on).

The play only "gets underway" following an elaborate dumb show which leads the audience through the coming play, depicting the poisoning of the king and the queen's subsequent marriage to the poisoner. This is a puzzle to any producer of "Hamlet": since Claudius self-indictment is dependent on his **surprise** at the poisoning/marriage, seeing the dumb show in prologue will take any edge off of the shock. Our options include: 1) Claudius is too distracted to pay attention to the dumb show (And perhaps the assumption back in that period was that any dumb show would be a waste of time, so people tended to occupy themselves otherwise **anyway**.) 2) The dumbshow is performed in such an abstract and stylized manner that even **if** anyone paid attention, none could make heads or tails of it, or, my choice: 3) cut the dumb show.

As the conversation between the Player King and Queen unwinds, we can only guess at which "dozen or sixteen lines" Hamlet, himself, inserted into the text, See Bloom's "The Invention of the Human" for a thorough discussion of this.

Yes, once again, "love" is "rhymed with" the un-rhyming "prove." But I choose not to play that joke a second time.

Hamlet draws Horatio aside, convinced that he is now the only one who can be entrusted with the truth.

HAMLET
There is a play to-night before the king;
One scene of it comes near the circumstance
Which I have told thee of my father's death:
I prithee, when thou seest that act afoot,
Even with the very comment of thy soul
Observe mine uncle: if his occulted guilt
Do not itself unkennel in one speech,
It is a damned ghost that we have seen...

The audience arrives! And Hamlet plays the mad and jesting host, dangerously mocking Queen Gertrude's quick marriage to Claudius', and talking lewdly to Ophelia, offering to "lie in her lap."

The play gets underway, and the player-king, Gonzago, assures his Queen that (despite her denials) she will remarry after his death...

Player King
I do believe you think what now you speak;
But what we do determine oft we break...
For 'tis a question left us yet to prove,
Whether love lead fortune, or else fortune love...
So think thou wilt no second husband wed;
But die thy thoughts when thy first lord is dead.

The Player Queen insists at great length "Both here and hence pursue me lasting strife, If, once a widow, ever I be wife!..." *Which stirs Queen Gertrude's awkward observation,* "The lady protests too much, methinks."

Knocking Claudius Upside the Head

The films of "Hamlet" seem especially keen on elongating the sense of dread that creeps over the king, who only gradually becomes aware that he is watching his own story play out, yet Shakespeare actually **collapses** the action into a sharp 1-2 punch. Rather than allowing the marriage to play out over subsequent scenes, Hamlet injects the "reveal"... a "spoiler" in the exact instant of the poisoning. The scene works best when Claudius is blindsided all at once, with the searing sting of "WIFE!"

Hamlet's "Mousetrap" has successfully "caught the conscience of the king." With an odd disturbance that at the very least has been such a startling display of public awkwardness, the audience is (if not already suspicious) left with the lingering question of "what was that all about?"

While it is unlikely that these odd thoughts will lead people to connect Claudius to the death of the late king, should Hamlet kill Claudius now, the explanation of Claudius' guilt (backed by Horatio's confirmation) will make some sense out of what has otherwise been a strange, inexplicable incident, and it is unlikely that any movement to depose the new King Hamlet (the legitimate successor, **anyway**) would take hold, despite any complaints surrounding his murder of Claudius.

The contrast of friendships heading in opposite directions could hardly be more vivid. The intimate "thou" between Hamlet and Horatio gives way to the familiar "you" toward Rosencrantz and Guildenstern, and Hamlet's stern lecture is nothing short of hostile: "Why look you now, how unworthy a thing you make of me!... 'Sblood, do you think I am easier to be played on than a pipe? Call me what instrument you will, though you can fret me, yet you cannot play upon me." (It's a terrific, blistering attack, but it plays better when there's an actual Guildenstern on stage to trade lines with.)

Gonzago is murdered by his nephew, who pours poison into his ear, and Hamlet sees to it that the point is lost on no one:

HAMLET
He poisons him i' the garden for's estate. His name's Gonzago:… you shall see anon how the murderer gets the love of Gonzago's wife.

Claudius starts from his chair, crying out for lights and stumbling his way out of the room! Hamlet checks in with Horatio, who confirms witnessing (as did pretty much everybody else in the hall) the sharp disturbance of the king at the climax of the murder. Hamlet has his proof!

Rosencrantz and Guildenstern return, scolding Hamlet for offending his mother, who now wishes to speak with him. Hamlet scorns Guildenstern for attempting to "play him like a pipe," before heading off to the Queen's closet (which is a much larger room than it probably sounds).

Nero and Claudius

The allusion to Nero resonates with this situation in several ways. Nero's mother, Agrippina, marrying for the third time, wed her own uncle (Nero's granduncle), whose name happened to be "Claudius." Shakespeare almost certainly had this in mind when inserting a Roman name into this Norse legend (about a king originally known as "Amleth"), especially given the repeated patterns of incest running through Nero's story.

Soon after Claudius was poisoned (probably by Agrippina), Nero, having married his step-sister (Claudius' daughter), took over the rule of Rome at the age of 17 (in 54 A.D.). Nero conducted several romantic affairs, threatening to divorce Claudia, as he and his mother fought over control of the empire. She attempted to have Nero supplanted by Brittanicus (Claudius' son from his first marriage), who conveniently died the day before he would have come of age. probably poisoned by Nero). Four years after taking the throne, with Agrippina meddling in his affairs, Nero attempted to have her drowned at sea. When that failed, he sent assassins to kill her. Legend has it that she requested to be stabbed in the belly that bore such a wicked son.

The Accelerator and the Brakes

Amid echoes of Nero's bloodthirsty reign, and with certain knowledge of his Uncle's guilt, Hamlet simultaneously attempts to work himself up to kill his uncle while restraining himself from reckless slaughter of his mother. Hamlet repeatedly resonates with echoes of fratricide (as it cites Cain & Abel), and matricide (in reference to Nero & Agrippina).

Just as Hamlet is ready to pounce on Claudius with his furious bloodlust, the demands from his mother (relayed by Rosencrantz and Guildenstern) divide Hamlet's energies between the accelerator (killing the king) and the brakes (sparing his mother).

It is important that Hamlet is clear that he DOES NOT intend to kill his mother – he will NOT be "unnatural," he will use NO dagger, and his soul will NEVER consent to the killing – but, with the tongue lashing that he intends to give, it should also be clear that it may be a struggle to hold this impulse in check.

It may well be that this act of keeping his rage in check, struggling to pull himself up short of killing, puts Hamlet in the disposition wherein he will hesitate when presented with the opportunity as he discovers Claudius at prayer.

Rosencrantz and Guildenstern, acting as pawns unwittingly caught up in the thick of a deadly game, have led Hamlet into a horrible misstep. Hamlet will ultimately take his revenge for their interference, as well as the several other irritations they have stirred.

BREAKNECK HAMLET

The only thing you need to know to understand this soliloquy is that the Roman Emperor, Nero, is famous for having had his own mother put to death.

HAMLET
Tis now the very witching time of night,
When churchyards yawn and hell itself breathes out
Contagion to this world: now could I drink hot blood,
And do such bitter business as the day
Would quake to look on. Soft! now to my mother.
O heart, lose not thy nature; let not ever
The soul of Nero enter this firm bosom:
Let me be cruel, not unnatural:
I will speak daggers to her, but use none;
My tongue and soul in this be hypocrites;
How in my words soever she be shent,
To give them seals never, my soul, consent!

Claudius: Trapped

One might argue that Claudius sounds not only like Lady Macbeth ("Out, damned spot! Out I say."), but also like Macbeth himself: "Will all great Neptune's ocean wash this blood clean from my hand?" I choose to connect him to "Lady M," in one sense because her compulsive blood-washing is better known, but also because it continues to underline Claudius' uncertain sexuality.

This play continues to be steeped in very Catholic notions of sin, guilt and forgiveness. Claudius, following his very public breakdown, is raked with guilt over the mortal sin of murdering his brother. Meanwhile, the late King Hamlet is burning in Purgatory for what we can only assume are less egregious sins.

The coming scene will hinge on the sincerity of Claudius' plea for forgiveness. And, in fact, the play's resolution will eventually hinge on Hamlet receiving (reciprocal) forgiveness from Laertes before dying.

Claudius' problem is that any form of forgiveness (and release from the guilty nightmare he now suffers), is dependent on his willingness to confess and release all of the ill-gotten gains (the crown, the kingdom, the position, the riches and the Queen) obtained through commission of the original sin.

Of course, it is no longer that simple. Renouncing all of these worldly goods would only get Claudius halfway there. Only the confession of the late king's murder would earn him Heavenly forgiveness, but that would likely come with a horrible earthly punishment. Knowing that he doesn't dare risk that likely execution, what then would be the point of renouncing all of the material goods?

Besides which, Claudius really likes being king and he might actually be good at "kinging" too. In essence, he is paralyzed. He can't move backwards, and any forward movement sinks him deeper into the depths of his sin.

Trapped in this in-between world, I am portraying Claudius with an apoplectic quiver. Inspired by "what if this cursed hand were thicker than itself..." I've given Claudius' right hand a life of its own, trembling almost constantly.

Also I'm portraying Claudius with an effete, almost feminine attitude. After waiting until middle age to marry, he proceeded to marry his brother's wife, probably for reasons more political than romantic. And calling out his nephew as "unmanly" in open court (Act I, Scene 2) strikes me as pointing to a very likely insecurity of his own in that area... Perhaps Shakespeare understood the psychological phenomena of "projection" long before psychologists coined the term.

ACT III, SCENE III. A room in the castle.

Sounding a little bit like Lady Macbeth, Claudius wrestles with his guilt...

KING CLAUDIUS
O, my offence is rank it smells to heaven;
It hath the primal eldest curse upon't,
A brother's murder...
What if this cursed hand
Were thicker than itself with brother's blood,
Is there not rain enough in the sweet heavens
To wash it white as snow?...
But, O, what form of prayer
Can serve my turn? 'Forgive me my foul murder'?
That cannot be; since I am still possess'd
Of those effects for which I did the murder...
Bow, stubborn knees; and, heart with strings of steel,
Be soft as sinews of the newborn babe!
All may be well.
[(Retires and kneels)]

Enter Hamlet.

Hamlet's Fatal Flaw

Here we find Hamlet making his one crucial, perhaps unforgiveable mistake. However it happens that fate, coincidence, or God has placed the motive, means and opportunity into Hamlet's hands to administer justice to Claudius, Hamlet's decision **not** to proceed is based, not on his own sense of virtue, but on his own desire to guarantee Claudius' ultimate damnation.

In other words, Hamlet has chosen to play God, a presumption which lies outside of mankind's purview. From a strictly Catholic point of view, this is a sin of "hubris" (pride): worse, perhaps, even than the actual killing of Claudius, and any and all troubles Hamlet encounters for the rest of the play can be traced from this single moment.

Of course, given that this is a one-man play, I have to abandon my portrayal of Claudius (during "Enter Hamlet") to assume the person of Hamlet. I leave a special light focused center stage, where Claudius had been kneeling to remind the audience that this character is still there, praying.

Normally, we would regard this speech as an "aside," but with no "scene" between the two men (a stage direction suggests Claudius has "retired" out of the focus of the scene) this speech is often described as a "soliloquy."

In performance, I cannot resist an in-joke that perhaps only a classically-trained actor would appreciate... When Hamlet says "That would be scanned," I play upon the secondary meaning that the word "scanned" has to anyone who plays Shakespeare, which is to "scan" a line of verse for the iambic rhythm. In doing so, we usually over-stress the stressed syllables, thus testing out the intended rhythm which lies beneath the lines.

As such I, as Hamlet, gesture sequentially to Claudius, to the imagined ghost of my father (whom I envision downstage right, where I originally "saw" him in Act I, Scene 4), and to myself, while reciting "a **VILL**ain **KILLS** my **FATH**er, **AND** for **THAT**, I **HIS** sole **SON** do **THIS** same **VILL**ain **SEND** to **HEAV**en?!" (I have no idea if anyone but me will ever get this joke, but I live in hope that one lone audience member will find it hysterical.)

The image of "heels kicking" at Heaven does not play as well on the page as it does on the stage. But with Claudius kneeling, it is easy to imagine his legs flailing upwards as Hamlet "trips" him, a gesture Hamlet can suggest with his arms... which then turns more sinister as Hamlet's gesture continues slowly forward to direct Claudius' soul downward, roaring "to Hell whereto it goes."

And, of course, the greatest irony of all: Claudius' attempt to pray was a wretched failure. Had Hamlet followed through on his impulse, he would undoubtedly have sent his uncle straight to hell.

HAMLET
Now might I do it pat, now he is praying;
And now I'll do't. And so he goes to heaven;
And so am I revenged. That would be scann'd:
A villain kills my father; and for that,
I, his sole son, do this same villain send
To heaven.
O, this is hire and salary, not revenge.
He took my father grossly, full of bread;
With all his crimes broad blown, as flush as May;
And how his audit stands who knows save heaven?
But in our circumstance and course of thought,
'Tis heavy with him: and am I then revenged,
To take him in the purging of his soul,
When he is fit and season'd for his passage?
No!
Up, sword; and know thou a more horrid hent:
When he is drunk asleep, or in his rage,
Or in the incestuous pleasure of his bed;
At gaming, swearing, or about some act
That has no relish of salvation in't;
Then trip him, that his heels may kick at heaven,
And that his soul may be as damn'd and black
As hell, whereto it goes. My mother stays:
This physic but prolongs thy sickly days.

KING CLAUDIUS
My words fly up, my thoughts remain below:
Words without thoughts never to heaven go.

Misdirected Fury

Hamlet's pendulum of impassioned decision-making seems to swing him toward vengeance at exactly the wrong moment. He paused to think when he should have acted, and, here, he acts where he should pause to think.

*Perhaps a single second's thought is all he would need to realize that the man behind the arras cannot be the king! Hamlet left the king behind, heading directly from there to the Queen's Closet. Claudius would need to have **raced past him** in the hallway to get behind the arras before Hamlet's arrival!*

*Hamlet launches into a devastating accusation of Gertrude: "Almost as bad, good mother, as kill a king and marry with his brother." Hamlet implicates GERTRUDE with the murder! Does he really think that Gertrude killed his father? Is he going "over the top" to force Gertrude to pay attention? This is, after all, the first time that we see anyone telling Gertrude that her husband was the victim of murder, and Hamlet leaps **far past** what we believe to be true, to suggest that she is, at the very least, complicit.*

Hamlet, raging with passion after his failure to kill Claudius, exhibits no remorse over the death of Polonius. To be fair, Hamlet has good reason to resent the meddlesome Polonius, who tore him away from his lover, Ophelia.

Clearly, Hamlet's memories of his father have been enhanced in retrospect. Certainly his father is the better man compared to Claudius, but Hamlet's celebration of his late father spirals into unlikely hyperbole, most likely stirred by the hatred and disgust he feels towards his uncle.

In performance, I pantomime two hand-sized portraits to hold up in Gertrude's face, always "elevating" the late King Hamlet, by holding his portrait higher in the air ("new lighted on a heaven-kissing hill") while absurdly disparaging Claudius as a "mildewed ear." This speech, more than anything, may call into question the reliability of Hamlet as a narrator. We may assume that Shakespeare put more of his own wit, intelligence and genius into the character of Hamlet than any other, and yet Hamlet's opinion might not be relied upon as Shakespeare's absolute voice. Shakespeare's genius still holds some advantage over this, his most thoroughly developed character.

In the context of this one-person play, I exploit the audience to choose a "Gertrude" in the front row, mercilessly accusing her of the sins Hamlet sees in his mother. I then pick out a young woman or an intimate couple, perhaps holding hands in the audience, as examples of "flaming youth" and "compulsive ardor," and giving them permission to "let virtue be as wax."

ACT III, SCENE IV. The Queen's closet.

Polonius alerts Gertrude that Hamlet is approaching, and, once again, hides behind the arras to listen in. Hamlet and Gertrude argue, and as their confrontation gets physical, Polonius cries out for help! Hamlet, thinking that he has caught the king amid an act of treachery, stabs Polonius... in the arras!

HAMLET

How now! a rat? Dead, for a ducat, dead!...
A bloody deed! almost as bad, good mother,
As kill a king, and marry with his brother...
Thou wretched, rash, intruding fool, farewell!
I took thee for thy better: take thy fortune;
...Look here, upon this picture, and on this,
The counterfeit presentment of two brothers.
See, what a grace was seated on this brow;
Hyperion's curls; the front of Jove himself;
An eye like Mars, to threaten and command;
A station like the herald Mercury
New-lighted on a heaven-kissing hill;
A combination and a form indeed,
Where every god did seem to set his seal,
To give the world assurance of a man:
This was your husband. Look you now, what follows:
Here is your husband; like a mildew'd ear,
Blasting his wholesome brother. Have you eyes?
Could you on this fair mountain leave to feed,
And batten on this moor? Ha! have you eyes?
You cannot call it love; for at your age
The hey-day in the blood is tame, it's humble,
And waits upon the judgment: and what judgment
Would step from this to this? Sense, sure, you have,
Else could you not have motion; but sure, that sense
Is apoplex'd; for madness would not err,
Nor sense to ecstasy was ne'er so thrall'd
But it reserved some quantity of choice,
To serve in such a difference. What devil was't
That thus hath cozen'd you at hoodman-blind?
Eyes without feeling, feeling without sight,
Ears without hands or eyes, smelling sans all,
Or but a sickly part of one true sense
Could not so mope.
O shame! where is thy blush? Rebellious hell,
If thou canst mutine in a matron's bones,
To flaming youth let virtue be as wax,

Frost Itself
Hamlet is either intentionally twisting the knife, here, to shame and horrify Gertrude, or he is entirely ignorant of female sexuality. Certainly Gertrude, newly remarried, would like to fancy herself a sexually attractive woman, still near her prime. While Hamlet's puritanical streak (or a patriarchal society), may account for some of his scorn, it is hard to imagine Hamlet reacting to Gertrude's sexuality at all were it not for the fact that she, his own mother, had married his uncle (taking the kingship from him in the process).

Of course, some psychologists suggest that Hamlet's overreaction is the result of an Oedipal desire for his mother, but it might just as easily be that, having just killed one man, Hamlet is feeling reckless and overwrought over losing his "window" to safely kill Claudius. (It is, at least, worth noting that Hamlet's priorities inspire fewer than seven lines railing against Claudius' murder of his father, and about forty lines criticizing his mother's poor judgment!)

The Polonial Setback
There's something a little bit "badass" about Hamlet in the line, "...to punish me with this and this with me." In that moment, Hamlet "owns" his own danger, essentially saying, "This is what happens when you screw with me; I am a punishment sent from heaven."

"Cruel only to be kind..." seems to be Hamlet's version of "tough love" over Gertrude, who has been reduced to the role of petulant child. Shakespeare often ends scenes or acts with a rhyming couplet, perhaps to cue audience applause (or to cue actors awaiting their entrance). Hamlet's use of the kind/behind rhyming couplet effectively ends the scene with Gertrude. (In the full play, she is left somewhat dazed at the sight of Hamlet conversing with an invisible ghost.) In performance, I treat the next ten lines as an extended aside to the audience, sharing information which he wouldn't want Gertrude to hear. He wouldn't want her to inform Claudius of his intent to "delve one yard below their mines and blow them at the moon." (He is, after all, still suspicious that Gertrude may have been complicit in the murder.)

As Hamlet delves "one yard below their mines" I have him ducking "below" to pantomime lifting the dead Polonius (rising up again on "blow them at the moon"). Most often Hamlet drags Polonius' body away, but with no actual body to drag, shouldering it in a lift makes a cleaner bit of pantomime.

This man shall set me packing.
Polonius' murder now forces Hamlet to bow to Claudius' demands to travel to England. Killing one man might be seen as an impulse of madness, but now killing the king would label Hamlet a serial killer, boxing him out from ever rising to the kingship. (It will take until Act V for Hamlet to steel himself to kill Claudius, throwing concern for the likely fallout to the winds.)

And melt in her own fire: proclaim no shame
When the compulsive ardour gives the charge,
Since frost itself as actively doth burn
And reason panders will... Nay, but to lie
In the rank sweat of an enseamed bed,
Stew'd in corruption, honeying and making love
Over the nasty sty,--
...A murderer and a villain;
A slave that is not twentieth part the tithe
Of your precedent lord; a vice of kings;
A cutpurse of the empire and the rule,
That from a shelf the precious diadem stole,
And put it in his pocket!
...A king of shreds and patches,--

*The Ghost returns, reminding Hamlet of his unfulfilled promise... and warning
him to lay-off of his mother...! Hamlet, having now killed a man, cannot kill yet
another, especially not the King, with impunity, and must thereby obey the
orders to travel to England with Rosencrantz and Guildenstern.*

HAMLET
Mother, for love of grace...
Go not to mine uncle's bed;
Assume a virtue, if you have it not.
...For this same lord,
I do repent: but heaven hath pleased it so,
To punish me with this and this with me...
I will bestow him, and will answer well
The death I gave him. So, again, good night.
I must be cruel, only to be kind:
Thus bad begins and worse remains behind...
There's letters seal'd: and my two schoolfellows,
Whom I will trust as I will adders fang'd,
They bear the mandate; they must sweep my way,
And marshal me to knavery. Let it work;
For 'tis the sport to have the engineer
Hoist with his own petard: and 't shall go hard
But I will delve one yard below their mines,
And blow them at the moon...
This man shall set me packing:
I'll lug the guts into the neighbour room.
Mother, good night. Indeed this counsellor
Is now most still, most secret and most grave,
Who was in life a foolish prating knave...

Catching his breath

Once I had finally managed to memorize through this point, I became acutely aware of just what an athletic feat Act III must be for any actor playing Hamlet. The act leads off with the greatest soliloquy ever, proceeds to Hamlet's impassioned takedown of Ophelia (and her spies), launches into a diatribe about acting, teeters over the opportunity to kill the king, and finishes with Hamlet laying into his mother, killing a man and carrying off the dead body (leaving the actor mostly drenched in sweat by the time all is done). He doesn't actually get to take Act IV "off," per se – In addition to some chasing around with Rosencrantz and Guildenstern, he has another major soliloquy: "How all occasions do inform against me" – but comparatively speaking, this is "downtime."

Aside from Act I, Scene I, in which Hamlet does not appear, he has dominated every scene of this play up until now. But here, at last, we have a scene without Hamlet at all, a phenomenon which will repeat in scenes 5, 6 & 7. Of course, this is explained by his departure to England, though what gets the laugh in this instance is that, as a one-man show, there will be no such "catching of breath."

But even were there a full cast, the production can afford no slowdown at this point. With the possible exception of Scene 4 ("How all occasions...") Act IV stands as a series of quick scenes, as the interlocking gears of action seem to be turning all at once. Shakespeare seems to know that things had better speed up in the fourth act to keep the audience from getting restless, and directors need to adjust the pace accordingly.

Dispensing Justice

While the "political implications" Claudius faces include Hamlet's popularity, Claudius also happens to know that Polonius was in the Queen's Closet to spy under Claudius' own command, and any attempt to prosecute Hamlet might bring that fact to light. Thus, personally directing the execution of Hamlet will damage Claudius' standing, and yet, allowing the public to continue to see Hamlet at liberty will call Claudius' power and judgment into play.

Sending Hamlet into what seems like a benevolent (almost forgiving) exile takes the immediate pressure off of Claudius, all the while shielding him from any blame for what might happen to Hamlet while he is away. But Claudius must enact this immediately (just as he must also have Polonius dead body hastily packed off, out of the way), before the spectacle of a free Hamlet might incite the public to rise against him in demand of justice.

54

ACT IV! In which the actor playing Hamlet usually gets to catch his breath from the workout of Act III!

SCENE I. A room in the castle.
Gertrude informs Claudius that Hamlet has killed Polonius! Claudius, aware of the political implications, insists:

CLAUDIUS
The sun no sooner shall the mountains touch,
But we will ship him hence: and this vile deed
We must, with all our majesty and skill,
Both countenance and excuse.

Rosencrantz and Guildenstern

Given that Rosencrantz and Guildenstern were companions to Hamlet during childhood, they must have come from a fairly privileged family (or families) to begin with. Even the King and Queen seem overly-solicitous of the two men, entreating them to snoop on Hamlet when, by rights, they could simply order them to obey. One suspects that these two boy-men have never known a hard-day's labor in their lives.

We know that Horatio has left his studies behind at Wittenberg to attend to Hamlet, and yet the only similar reference to Rosencrantz and Guildenstern is Hamlet's allusion to "my two schoolfellows" (Act III, Scene 4), which may suggest that they, too, are back from Wittenburg, although, given their dim-witted ignorance, we may assume them to be C-students at best. (Or, perhaps, "schoolfellows" references their time in pre-school together.) They seem like spoiled wastrels, smart enough only to crack the occasional dirty joke, but unable to keep up with Hamlet's searing sarcasm... to which Hamlet notes, "A knavish speech sleeps in a foolish ear."

Hamlet no longer makes any effort to hide his resentment for Rosencrantz and Guildenstern. They have traded on their childhood friendship to suck up to the more powerful benefactor, the King. Though they have blundered into the middle of this conflict, it is their habit of meddling "above their pay grade," as it were, "marshaling Hamlet to knavery," which will nearly get Hamlet killed, an ignorant blunder for which Hamlet cannot forgive them. (Shakespeare clearly means to contrast these boot-lickers with Horatio, a man of no visible means who retains his loyalties and moral balance.)

Hamlet paints a stark symbiotic relationship: Rosencrantz and Guildenstern think they are using the King for their own advancement, while Hamlet knows that it is the King using them for his own. Hamlet's own view of Claudius suggests that he promises great favors with no intent to ever deliver: "... of the chameleon's dish: I eat the air, promise crammed." Like the chameleon whose tongue darts to catch and eat insects faster than the human eye might notice (so that it seems to live off of nothing but air), Hamlet sees Claudius' promise of the kingship as empty air. Hamlet will need to outlive Claudius to collect... and that prospect seems especially unlikely at the moment.

Alluding once again to the animal world, Hamlet turns Claudius into an ape. In portraying this, I outline the enormous jaw of the imagined ape with my hand, an inch or two from my own face, opening and closing the hand as if "chewing." This action works also for "squeezing you" as Rosencrantz and Guildenstern pass into the imagined gullet of the beast.

ACT IV, SCENE II. Another room in the castle.
Rosencrantz and Guildenstern catch up to Hamlet, who calls Rosencrantz "a sponge."

HAMLET
Ay, sir, that soaks up the king's countenance, his rewards, his authorities. But such officers do the king best service in the end: he keeps them, like an ape, in the corner of his jaw; first mouthed, to be last swallowed: when he needs what you have gleaned, it is but squeezing you, and, sponge, you shall be dry again.

Getting under Claudius' Skin

Hamlet's ability to taunt the King is masterful and astonishing. In very short order, he calls Claudius fat, he places worms and maggots above the king in authority (as "Emperors"), while reminding him that his death will find his remains every bit as defiled as the meanest beggar. Topping it off with a wit worthy of Noel Coward, he tells Claudius to "go to Hell," by seeking Polonius "in the other place yourself." (I work to portray Hamlet, here with a wide-eyed innocence, idly tracing the back of his neck with his finger.)

In performance, I twist the knife one more time, having Hamlet almost singing "up the stairs into the lobby," as he flounces his way off stage. In addition to the madness Hamlet is feigning, and the utter disregard for Claudius' attempts at gravity, I see him mocking Claudius uncomfortable masculinity with a fey sexual ambivalence.

This chapter of English history closely predates the telling of Shakespeare's History Plays, which pick up England's history around the year 1299. And some of the crucial roots of **that** story were planted in the year 1066, with the Norman Conquest. In other words, this tale from circa 1050 immediately predates much of the historical material with which we're already kind of familiar.* One wonders how very familiar Shakespeare was with these more obscure reaches of English history, given how much more familiar we are with those events from the Norman Conquest on forward... events that have crystalized in our imaginations, if only because Shakespeare's histories have popularized and fixed them in place for us.

Danish names of that time (such as "Sven," "Canute" and "Amleth") tend to sound a little goofy to our Anglo Saxon ears and, notably, Shakespeare chose the Roman "Claudius" for Hamlet's uncle, which probably had more to do with drawing a parallel to the tale of Nero (whose granduncle who eventually became his stepfather was also a "Claudius") than reflecting any Danish ancestral line.

As Claudius speaks to "England" it makes sense to address the audience seated before him, given that Shakespeare's contemporaneous audience was filled with immediate representatives of that nation, and my quivering gestures toward those present continues to reveal the "apoplexy" in Claudius' hand. Claudius' deliberate attempts to lay out a formal series of reminders is utterly abandoned as he is reduced to wailing his horrible command with "Do it, England!" amid a quivering white hot rage. As he cites the hectic that lives in his "blood," I envision his whole arm developing a life of its own, shaking with anger, a force of which only England can cure him.

---

* Also explored in my "Shakespeare's Histories; Ten Epic Plays at a Breakneck Pace"

ACT IV, SCENE III. Another room in the castle.

Claudius is faced with the same dilemma that Hamlet faces: the other is too popular with the people to be killed without greater provocation.

Hamlet arrives, informing Claudius that Polonius is "at supper."

HAMLET
Not where he eats, but where he is eaten: a certain convocation of politic worms are e'en at him. Your worm is your only emperor for diet: we fat all creatures else to fat us, and we fat ourselves for maggots: your fat king and your lean beggar is but variable service, two dishes, but to one table: that's the end... A man may fish with the worm that hath eat of a king, and eat of the fish that hath fed of that worm.

Claudius demands to know where Polonius is.

HAMLET
In heaven; send hither to see: if your messenger find him not there, seek him i' the other place yourself. But indeed, if you find him not within this month, you shall nose him as you go up the stairs into the lobby...

Claudius sends Rosencrantz and Guildenstern after Hamlet, insisting that they ship off for England tonight!

It might help to know that, in the year 950, Sven-the-forked-beard of Denmark conquered England, over which his son, Canute, ruled until 1035, after which, for a brief time, England was forced to pay tribute to Denmark, which was, essentially, stealing their lunch money, and extorting them into doing their dirty work. This sets the action of this play around the year 1050, and Claudius' next speech earns him exactly zero fans among the Elizabethan audience...

KING CLAUDIUS
And, England, if my love thou hold'st at aught--
As my great power thereof may give thee sense,
Since yet thy cicatrice looks raw and red
After the Danish sword, and thy free awe
Pays homage to us--thou mayst not coldly set
Our sovereign process; which imports at full,
By letters congruing to that effect,
The present death of Hamlet. Do it, England;
For like the hectic in my blood he rages,
And thou must cure me: till I know 'tis done,
Howe'er my haps, my joys were ne'er begun.

Hamlet Commits

As Fortinbras' army prepares, he sends his Captain on a mission to Elsinore for permission to march. The Captain encounters Hamlet, dropping derisive mention of the "little patch of ground" they go to fight for and Hamlet sends Rosencrantz and Guildenstern ahead, leaving him to deliver this piece as his sixth and final soliloquy.

Given that I am still breathing heavily from Claudius' fit of rage in Scene 3, I tend to find myself, against all better judgment, letting out "How all occasions do inform against me and spur my dull revenge" with a sigh. [I have railed for years against actors sighing on stage!] And yet, at Hamlet (and I) gathers his breath, the second sentence (through "a beast, no more") is a little longer, and the third sentence longer still. By the time Hamlet gets to "Now whether it be..." he is back in his fully-winded analytical mode, devising arguments that take eight lines of verse to develop. As the reality of the precarious Norse venture sets in, Hamlet envisions these men hurtling towards death "like beds," and is struck with outrage over his own seeming paralysis in light of their reckless abandon. The climax of the speech finds him worked up into his own raging fury, no longer undercutting himself with self-mockery such as "What an ass am I!" but playing through to the end in a full-throated battle cry.

But, is this **Shakespeare's** view? To my thinking, Shakespeare is depicting the ridiculous **futility** of such battle madness, such that even the brilliant Hamlet would envision himself fighting and dying over "an eggshell" or "a straw." The notion that ten thousand men would die over a patch of land not large enough to contain the corpses of the combatants is a patently absurd and a shocking undervaluing of the life of man, who is, after all, "like a God."

In essence, Hamlet has succumbed to peer pressure: "If ten thousand men are ready to fight and die over nothing, why am I still standing here?"

The next time we see Hamlet, he will be a different man: more firm, more resolute, and readier to set his life at stake. While the Hamlet of Acts I-IV was waiting for his opening: wanting to kill Claudius, but only if he could ensure his own safety (and ultimate kingship) while doing it, the Hamlet who returns from the sea voyage (especially after uncovering the plot to put him to death), takes no more such precautions: His job is to kill Claudius, and he may only have a single second's opportunity to accomplish it. ("A man's life [is] no more than to say 'one.'")

If Hamlet can kill Claudius and live, so much the better. But with only one opportunity likely, Hamlet will return as a near-transcendent being, with an equanimity that rises above all mortal concern, putting his fate entirely in the "divinity that shapes our ends."

ACT IV, SCENE IV. A plain in Denmark.

Fortinbras' army marches its way across Denmark, and Hamlet, about to ship off for England, learns the land that they go to fight for in Poland is nothing but… "a little patch of ground / That hath in it no profit but the name."

HAMLET
How all occasions do inform against me,
And spur my dull revenge! What is a man,
If his chief good and market of his time
Be but to sleep and feed? a beast, no more.
Sure, he that made us with such large discourse,
Looking before and after, gave us not
That capability and god-like reason
To fust in us unused. Now, whether it be
Bestial oblivion, or some craven scruple
Of thinking too precisely on the event,
A thought which, quarter'd, hath but one part wisdom
And ever three parts coward, I do not know
Why yet I live to say 'This thing's to do;'
Sith I have cause and will and strength and means
To do't. Examples gross as earth exhort me:
Witness this army of such mass and charge
Led by a delicate and tender prince,
Whose spirit with divine ambition puff'd
Makes mouths at the invisible event,
Exposing what is mortal and unsure
To all that fortune, death and danger dare,
Even for an egg-shell. Rightly to be great
Is not to stir without great argument,
But greatly to find quarrel in a straw
When honour's at the stake. How stand I then,
That have a father kill'd, a mother stain'd,
Excitements of my reason and my blood,
And let all sleep? while, to my shame, I see
The imminent death of twenty thousand men,
That, for a fantasy and trick of fame,
Go to their graves like beds, fight for a plot
Whereon the numbers cannot try the cause,
Which is not tomb enough and continent
To hide the slain? O, from this time forth,
My thoughts be bloody, or be nothing worth!

Distraction

While I make light of it here, there is little that is amusing in Ophelia's condition, and most productions depict her as seriously disturbed, unkempt, and sexually voracious... sharing more of the traits of a disturbed vagrant than the daughter of nobility.

Dominated and dictated to by a series of overbearing male figures for her entire life, the sudden death of her father and rejection by her lover (amid the seeming abandonment of her brother) has left Ophelia wracked by guilt, anguish and desperation.

Laertes spends the latter acts of this play with a chip on his shoulder, conscious of every slight, seemingly ready to duel on a moment's notice. To us, the modern audience, this seems like a hotheaded overreaction. And yet, to these devout Catholics, any and every shortcut around the rites and rituals of the church's process of internment was a dangerous flirtation with eternal damnation. Any perceived or actual slight of the dead (as first performed upon Laertes' father and, soon, his sister) would point to an afterlife even more "horrible" than the fires of purgatory currently endured by Hamlet's father.

Sometimes, it's best just not to swear

At first glance, Claudius' promises to Laertes seem to be simple hyperbole... the reflexive impulse of a desperate man. And yet, eventually we find that the "ax" to which Claudius alludes is no metaphor at all, but the very instrument Claudius has demanded that the English use on the neck of Hamlet. (Claudius knows full well what Laertes does not: that he has already signed orders directing Hamlet's execution.)

In Act V we will ultimately learn that those orders command England "not to stay [delay for] the grinding of the ax" before striking off Hamlet's head. The English audience, more familiar with such executions would know what a horrible, botched, bloody mess such an execution might make, and how long, drawn out and painful that process might be. Claudius is essentially ordering a bludgeoning and slicing torture, in **addition** to Hamlet's execution!

Even more significantly, however, Claudius' current pledge is predicated by "where the offense is..." And while Hamlet is certainly guilty of the death of Polonius, the real "offense" lies, secretly, at his own feet, and the metaphorical "ax" will fall upon himself. His bold promise not only predicts, but may inadvertently suggest to Laertes, the fate that is his due.

ACT IV, SCENE V. Elsinore. A room in the castle.

Following Hamlet's attack and her father's death, Ophelia has grown distracted, which seems to be the Elizabethan euphemism for "a little nutty." She visits distractedly with Gertrude, singing a song about a maid at her love's window on Valentine's day: The lover "Let in the maid, that out a maid / Never departed more." *The word "maid," back then, did not necessarily mean the woman who makes the bed.*

Laertes is back! Now at the head of a rabble, threatening to kill Claudius, who has given his father, Polonius, a quick, unceremonious burial while allowing Hamlet to roam free! Ophelia returns, singing more of her distracted songs while passing out flowers to everyone in the room. Claudius promises to give satisfaction to the agonizing Laertes, swearing "Where the offence is let the great axe fall."

Pirates!

For the modern audience, unfamiliar with the amenities and protocols surrounding capture by pirates on the open seas, this can be a difficult passage to navigate. (I've already removed several of the more confusing clauses.) The advantage that most theatres discover in placing the words directly into the mouth of Hamlet is that it brings us one layer closer to the action, as felt by someone who was engaged in the fighting. (Most of us, reading someone else's letters aloud, lack the impassioned inflection of an author describing his own experiences.)

In simple terms, a well-armed pirate ship caught up to Hamlet's vessel, and amid the fight, Hamlet leapt, or swung across to their ship (escaping a death that he already knew awaited him in England), just as they broke away and sailed off, either defeated in the fight, or, perhaps, victorious in claiming the richest prisoner on board... or, perhaps, carried away in the opposite direction by a sudden gust of wind.

There is something ominous about "of them I have much to tell thee," and I always treat this as a sly afterthought: Hamlet picks up his quill to write this addendum to a letter that is otherwise completed. Perhaps fifty percent of the audience has at least heard the title of the play, "Rosencrantz and Guildenstern are Dead," and the portentous tone of Hamlet's sudden gravity in such a moment will, for that group, resonate with a sense of what is coming.

ACT IV, SCENE VI. Another room in the castle.
Sailors bring Horatio a secret letter from Hamlet, and Horatio reads it aloud (though more often than not, this is where we pipe in Hamlet in voiceover).

HORATIO (or HAMLET)
...Ere we were two days old at sea, a pirate of very warlike appointment gave us chase... and in the grapple I boarded them: on the instant they got clear of our ship; so I alone became their prisoner. They have dealt with me like thieves of mercy: but... repair thou to me with as much speed as thou wouldst fly death. I have words to speak in thine ear will make thee dumb... Rosencrantz and Guildenstern hold their course for England: of them I have much to tell thee...

The Return of Noel Coward

The payoff of having Hamlet speak his own letters, lies in the very different tone Hamlet takes with the King. We may recognize "Hamlet-as-Noel-Coward," steeped in sarcasm with "high and mighty," "your kingdom," and "your kingly eyes..." sharp tweaks to the king Hamlet knows deserves no such high regard.

Hamlet's "set naked on your kingdom" originally struck me as metaphorical (naked as "without means or protection"), but upon further consideration seems literal: As the pirates escaped with Hamlet, alone, they would certainly have stolen the clothing of the ship's richest passenger. But "naked" **also** strikes me as another jab at Claudius. Hamlet seems to know that this awkward image will trigger a strange short-circuit within Claudius, whose immediate response to this letter is his curious/appalled/intrigued exclamation, "Naked?"

All of these plans are, of course, thick with irony for anyone already familiar with the play's end. They may well manage to kill Hamlet with this opportunistic intrigue, but as Horatio explains at the end, they are "in this upshot..." shooting their ammunition upwards which will ultimately "fall on the inventors' heads."

Gertrude's depiction, dazzlingly lyrical, is worth quoting in full:

> GERTRUDE
> There is a willow grows aslant a brook,
> That shows his hoar leaves in the glassy stream;
> Of crow-flowers, nettles, daisies, and long purples
> That liberal shepherds give a grosser name,
> But our cold maids do dead men's fingers call them:
> There, on the pendant boughs her coronet weeds
> Clambering to hang, an envious sliver broke;
> When down her weedy trophies and herself
> Fell in the seeping brook. Her clothes spread wide;
> And, mermaid-like, awhile they bore her up:
> Which time she chanted snatches of old tunes;
> As one incapable of her own distress,
> Or like a creature native and indued
> Unto that element: but long it could not be
> Till that her garments, heavy with their drink,
> Pull'd the poor wretch from her melodious lay
> To muddy death.

"Laertes is angry" is, of course, ironic understatement to his actual insistence: "I have a speech of fire that fain would blaze but that this folly [weeping] douts [douses] it."

ACT IV, SCENE VII. Another room in the castle.
Claudius convinces Laertes that Hamlet is an enemy to them both, and a messenger arrives with another letter from Hamlet!

KING CLAUDIUS (or HAMLET)
'High and mighty, You shall know I am set naked on your kingdom. To-morrow shall I beg leave to see your kingly eyes: when I shall... recount the occasion of my sudden and more strange return.

Claudius has a plan: he will propose a fencing match between Laertes and Hamlet, and Hamlet won't be able to resist the challenge! Meanwhile, Laertes can sneak in an "unbated" sword... one without the little button on the end to prevent the blade from piercing the skin.

Laretes does Claudius one better! It just so happens that he has bought a bit of poison of late! He will dip the tip of his blade into it so that, with even the slightest scratch, it will kill Hamlet!

Claudius has yet another idea! Just in case both plans fail, he'll prepare a chalice with poison added to the wine, so that, should Hamlet, exhausted from his workout, call out for drink... they'll have him coming and going!

Queen Gertrude reports that Ophelia, amid her distraction, fell into a brook, and floated along for a while (singing her strange songs), at least until her clothing became saturated, and "pulled the poor wretch from her melodious lay to muddy death."

Laertes is angry.

Whistling in the Graveyard

Shakespeare lists the Gravedigger as a "Clown," which may suggest the intended tone of this scene. He was likely played by the most playful improviser of the cast, who would likewise be amongst the performers needing the greatest restraint, warned to "speak no more than is set down for them."

The scene continues in a comic vein as Hamlet (who has yet to learn what we already know about Ophelia's death) trades quips with the Gravedigger, while brilliantly "riffing" on the possible lives of the several skulls that the Clown tosses up out of the grave. Once again, Shakespeare brings Hamlet to contemplate the abyss, but this time joking wildly in the face of death, not realizing the "one-two punch" that is about to hit him:

First, Hamlet is reminded of the death of Yorick, the one person he may have loved even more than his father or Ophelia. Any joy brought up by those memories, however, will be quickly destroyed by news of the death of Ophelia, a love he was never able to fully acknowledge while she was alive.

Unwittingly, Hamlet has tied these deaths together as, teasing the remains of Yorick, he directs him to "my lady's [Ophelia's] chamber." In telling her to "paint an inch thick," he echoes his previous scorn of the "paintings" that women wear, amid the relentless torment of "Get thee to a nunnery." Moments before learning of her death, he has recalled his greatest act of cruelty toward Ophelia, joking that no matter how thickly Ophelia may pile on her makeup, it will ultimately rot away, leaving nothing but a skull.

The most misquoted line in all of Shakespeare

"Alas, poor Yorick, I knew him, Horatio," cannot be delivered without at least half of the audience thinking that the actor playing Hamlet has screwed up his line, oddly replacing the word "well" with "Horatio." (The second most misquoted line is either "The lady protests too much, methinks" from Act III, or "Out damned spot" from Macbeth.)

The span since Yorick's death forces us to question "How old is Hamlet, anyway?" Assuming that Hamlet was 6-10 years old in the days he played so fondly with the King's Jester... adding 23 years places this (assumedly late-teens/early 20s college student) somewhere oddly in the range of 29-33.

There are at least two schools of thought around this:
1) As Harold Bloom puts forward, Shakespeare is suggesting that Hamlet's voyage to England has somehow "aged" him; the resolve, the readiness to die, the lack of concern over the desperation of his plight, the almost mystical one-ness with his fate is echoed by this notion that Hamlet has somehow aged some ten years beyond our expectations. Or...
2) Shakespeare forgot.

ACT V

SCENE I. A churchyard.
Two gravediggers question why Ophelia is being given the preferential treatment of a Christian burial when it seems fairly evident that her death was the result of a suicide. The answer: because she's rich and well connected.

Hamlet and Horatio come upon a gravedigger, singing while he works, tossing a skull on up out of the grave.

HAMLET
That skull had a tongue in it, and could sing once: how the knave jowls it to the ground, as if it were Cain's jaw-bone, that did the first murder! It might be the pate of a politician, which this ass now o'er-reaches; one that would circumvent God, might it not?...There's another: why may not that be the skull of a lawyer? Where be his quiddities now, his quillets, his cases, his tenures, and his tricks? why does he suffer this rude knave now to knock him about the sconce with a dirty shovel, and will not tell him of his action of battery? Hum! This fellow might be in's time a great buyer of land, with his statutes, his recognizances, his fines, his double vouchers, his recoveries: is this the fine of his fines, and the recovery of his recoveries, to have his fine pate full of fine dirt? will his vouchers vouch him no more of his purchases, and double ones too, than the length and breadth of a pair of indentures? The very conveyances of his lands will hardly lie in this box; and must the inheritor himself have no more, ha?

Hamlet asks how long a body will lie in the ground before it rots, and the grave-digger points out the unearthed skull of the king's former jester, Yorick, who died some twenty-three years before.

HAMLET
[Picking up the skull.] Alas, poor Yorick! I knew him, Horatio: a fellow of infinite jest, of most excellent fancy: he hath borne me on his back a thousand times; and now, how abhorred in my imagination it is! my gorge rims at it. Here hung those lips that I have kissed I know not how oft. Where be your gibes now? Your gambols? your songs? your flashes of merriment, that were wont to set the table on a roar? Not one now, to mock your own grinning? quite chap-fallen? Now get you to my lady's chamber, and tell her, let her paint an inch thick, to this favour she must come; make her laugh at that. Prithee, Horatio... Dost thou think Alexander looked o' this fashion i' the earth? ...And smelt so? pah!

Hamlet the Dane

Hamlet has worked himself up into a climax of silliness: Alexander and Caesar are, of course, two of the greatest conquerors that the world has known, and he mocks just how empty those great military victories were, "tracing the noble dust of Alexander" from glory to nothingness, as that body rots away until there is nothing left of the conqueror than what might "stop a beer barrel."

Shakespeare has set Hamlet up for a fall: his mockery turns to grief, and that grief turns to rage as he sees himself usurped as chief mourner for his love. We may only guess just how deeply Hamlet's love for Ophelia ran. It seems evident that the scorn he heaped upon her during "get thee to a nunnery" was an act, performed for the observers he knew were standing by, though one must assume the fierceness of his attack came at least partly from his realization that Ophelia was complicit in the charade. It also seems that Hamlet never reconciled with Ophelia: neither since the "nunnery" scene, nor since killing her father. These two events in quick succession had a horrible impact on her, to which Hamlet had seemed indifferent and that indifference must have contributed greatly to her ultimate breakdown.

One senses a taste of false bravado in this exchange with Laertes, almost as if Hamlet is more disturbed by Laertes' own play-acted grief which has stolen his moment of self-righteous mourning. There is something just a little too over-the-top about "This is I, Hamlet the Dane," which seems every bit as artificial as "This is a job for Superman!" After all, everyone else around him is also Danish, and with the exception, perhaps, of the gravediggers, they all probably already know that he is Hamlet. It's a bit of unnecessary melodrama that suggests Hamlet may be striking a pose deliberately.

Moreover, there is something further over-the-top about the two men leaping into the grave, claiming to want to be buried alive along with the corpse, and simultaneously attempting to throttle the other.

In the spirit of that extremity, I pantomime both participants in this fight, first as Laertes, with one hand on Hamlet's imagined throat, while the other hand struggles to peel Hamlet's imagined hand from his own. Then, shifting, one hundred eighty degrees and switching hands, as Hamlet, likewise strangling and struggling before the two find themselves being pulled apart, leaping backwards out of the grave.

... To what base uses we may return, Horatio! Why may
not imagination trace the noble dust of Alexander, till he find it stopping a
bung-hole?... as thus: Alexander died, Alexander was buried, Alexander
returneth into dust; the dust is earth; of earth we make loam; and why of that
loam, whereto he was converted, might they not stop a beer-barrel?
Imperious Caesar, dead and turn'd to clay,
Might stop a hole to keep the wind away:
O, that that earth, which kept the world in awe,
Should patch a wall to expel the winter flaw!

*A funeral procession arrives, and Hamlet observes the angry Laertes, arguing
with the priest about the minimized ceremony for his... sister! Hamlet is
stunned to realize that Ophelia has died, even as Laertes leaps into the grave!*

LAERTES
Hold off the earth awhile,
Till I have caught her once more in mine arms:
Now pile your dust upon the quick and dead,
Till of this flat a mountain you have made...!

Hamlet cannot take this lying down:

HAMLET
What is he whose grief
Bears such an emphasis? whose phrase of sorrow
Conjures the wandering stars, and makes them stand
Like wonder-wounded hearers? This is I,
Hamlet the Dane.

Hamlet leaps into the grave too. The men grapple.

LAERTES
The devil take thy soul!

HAMLET
Thou pray'st not well.
I prithee, take thy fingers from my throat;
...hold off thy hand.

The Attendants part the two, and pull them out of the grave.

I Loved Ophelia!

Not to sell him entirely short: I believe that Hamlet does, indeed love Ophelia, and this affirmation is certainly Hamlet's first public acknowledgement thereof. We may recall that Gertrude and Claudius were unaware of Hamlet's affection for her when Polonius told them about it in Act II. Polonius, himself, only knew by rumor that Hamlet had "given private time" to her. Thus, this bold declaration is a decisive move in light of his previous silence. But whether Hamlet would indeed follow through, allowing himself to "be buried quick with her" (or whether it is another pose), is an open question.

Regardless, I find that when "I LOVED OPHELIA" rings out as three, resounding, fully committed words, there is something transformative in the speaking itself, a shift within Hamlet that surfaces in the process of the speaking: an honest passion that manifests in this public declaration.

Cut from this variation of the scene are Hamlet's and Laertes' oblique references to mountains that most of us have never heard of, which would be dwarfed ("Make Ossa like a wart!") by the amount of ground each man would insist be piled upon him. One may wonder if those mountains would be tributes to Ophelia or to the men who insist that they love her...

HAMLET (*Continued.*)
I loved Ophelia: forty thousand brothers
Could not, with all their quantity of love,
Make up my sum.
…Dost thou come here to whine?
To outface me with leaping in her grave?
Be buried quick with her, and so will I…
Let Hercules himself do what he may,
The cat will mew and dog will have his day.

A divinity that shapes our ends

Hamlet describes the key incident which has led to his profound character shift. The letter reveals, beyond what Hamlet was already sure of (that Claudius killed his father), and what he may think is probable (that Claudius, fears and despises Hamlet), that Claudius is actively plotting to have him killed. This cat-and-mouse game now is being played for keeps on both sides. The stark realization of this is a violent jar to all of Hamlet's assumptions. As mentioned, The implications of "not to stay the grinding of the ax" cannot be understated. The duller the blade, the more ugly, painful and protracted the execution.

We may assume that Claudius had insisted that Hamlet get away from Denmark "for his own good." The killing of Polonius has stirred some insurrection among the people (not the least being Laertes), and Hamlet needs to get out of the country for a while "until things cool down."

This was not an "exile," as Claudius probably would have assured him, but a "diplomatic mission," to see to it that England continues to pay the tribute that is currently in arrears. England, of course, could be expected to treat him with all of the honors due to a visiting prince: state dinners, parties and companionship. Perhaps a marriage to an English princess was envisioned to solidify the partnership between the two countries. It is a vacation, surely, with "benefits..." a bit of romantic intrigue on the side.

Certainly all of this might be on the table as a vague or explicit promise to Hamlet, all of which he, more than likely, entirely disbelieved. Much more likely, this was an **implicit** exile: England would be told, "Here is Hamlet: keep him occupied for a while. Show him around. Give him the tour of the country. Take him up to Scotland or over to Ireland for a visit there, but whatever you do, don't let him come back! Find an excuse not to let him return for the next year or two or five. We'll let you know when things settle down back here."

Thus, between "My head should be struck off" and "I sat me down..." a transition occurs within Hamlet. There is no longer any room for passive indecisiveness. Only a vague, idle inquisitiveness alerted Hamlet of the high stakes for which he was now playing. He could no longer drift along without taking firm, resolute action, and his first targets would be those two childhood companions who betrayed him by siding with the king: thus Hamlet, yet unaware that the next morning would bring an attack from a pirate ship and the opportunity to escape, devises the plan to have them "hoist with their own petard."

Horatio recognizes this sudden coldness in Hamlet, evident in the delicacy with which he questions and reminds him. Horatio is clearly the one man on Hamlet's good side, but all of a sudden it has become clear that Hamlet is no longer a man to be toyed with.

ACT V, SCENE II. A hall in the castle.

Hamlet tells Horatio of the voyage to England. Some presentiment kept him awake... sneaking out to where Rosencrantz and Guildenstern slept, digging out the letter dictating the orders to England.

HAMLET
There's a divinity that shapes our ends,
Rough-hew them how we will.
Up from my cabin...in the dark
Groped I to find...
Their grand commission; ...an exact command,
Larded with many several sorts of reasons
...That, on the supervise, no leisure bated,
No, not to stay the grinding of the axe,
My head should be struck off.
...I sat me down,
Devised a new commission, wrote it fair:
...That, on the view and knowing of these contents,
Without debatement further, more or less,
He should the bearers put to sudden death.
...Subscribed it, gave't the impression, placed it safely,
The changeling never known...

Horatio notes, "So Guildenstern and Rosencrantz go to't?"

The pass and fell incensed points

We learn of the events at sea in reverse order to their occurrence. **First** Hamlet found the letter, and **then** he took advantage of the pirate attack to escape the fate which he now knew awaited him. It was by pure luck that Hamlet read the commission and escaped via the pirate ship, and Hamlet will trust luck to place opportunity into his hands once again. He may only get a single second, but this time, he will not let the moment of revenge pass. In my performance, Hamlet snaps his fingers on "one," representing the single second's opportunity to put Claudius to death. Claudius, not knowing what Hamlet has done, must bide his time, which leaves this brief "interim" for Hamlet to take action.

There is a kind of a perfect balance and perfect peace within Hamlet. We sense him ready to take whatever life brings him, whether to live or to die. He is poised and, in a sense, perhaps, has already beaten Claudius... taking everything Claudius could throw at him and surviving with his integrity intact.

This speech to Laertes is shockingly transcendent. Hamlet recognizes the wrong he has done Laertes and the venom that Claudius has inspired within Laertes. Hamlet begs Laerte's pardon cleanly, if not entirely honestly. His madness was, after all, always put-on. And though Laertes may have heard of Hamlet's "sore distraction," that distraction, itself, was a lie.

Yet when we look at the exact wrongs Hamlet performed against Laertes: scorning his sister, killing his father, and grappling with him in the grave, Hamlet **was** caught up in a literal "distraction:" panic over Polonius' spying, fury towards Claudius and grief over the loss of Ophelia. Hamlet is not lying about **that**, and it is the very sincerity that Hamlet radiates which will sway Laertes back to Hamlet's side in his dying moments.

Of course, as the men choose their weapons and Claudius sets out wine, the audience is already in on the plot between Claudius and Laertes and may expel some nervous laughter to dispel some of the highly-charged tension.

The actual dialogue that Shakespeare provides leaves some confusion over the exact number of cups of wine, as Claudius drinks from one, and places a "pearl" in a cup as a special prize for Hamlet. In some productions, he does this to the same cup from which he has just drunk, and so, perhaps it is the pearl, itself, that has been dipped in poison. This is, of course, too much to explain as we thunder toward the climax, so I work from the assumption of multiple glasses.

For most productions, the Hamlet/Laertes duel is the highlight of the play, and these three exchanges are realized in several minutes of elaborate swordplay. And yet, any such choreography with one man pantomiming, alone, will quickly descend into farce, and so I play these "touches" at a modern competitive pace, with each exchange concluded in the span of perhaps a single second.

HAMLET
Why, man, they did make love to this employment;
They are not near my conscience:
...'Tis dangerous when the baser nature comes
Between the pass and fell incensed points
Of mighty opposites.

Horatio reminds Hamlet that news from England will get back to Claudius soon.

HAMLET
It will be short: the interim is mine;
And a man's life's no more than to say 'One.'
...There's a special providence in the fall of a sparrow. If it be now, 'tis not to come; if it be not to come, it will be now; if it be not now, yet it will come: the readiness is all: since no man has aught of what he leaves, what is't to leave betimes?

Claudius and the rest of the court arrive for the grand fencing match, and Hamlet offers his hand to Laertes.

HAMLET
Give me your pardon, sir:
...You must needs have heard, how I am punish'd
With sore distraction.
...Was't Hamlet wrong'd Laertes? Never Hamlet:
If Hamlet from himself be ta'en away,
And when he's not himself does wrong Laertes...
Who does it, then? His madness: if't be so,
Hamlet is of the faction that is wrong'd;
His madness is poor Hamlet's enemy...

The two men choose their weapons, and Claudius sets out cups of wine for their anticipated celebration afterwards.

On the first pass, Hamlet scores a touch on Laertes, and Claudius drinks to Hamlet, while indicating the special cup that awaits him. Hamlet puts off drinking, while scoring a second touch against Laertes, and this time Queen Gertrude, "carousing to your fortune!" reaches for Hamlet's cup, drinking before Claudius can stop her: "Gertrude, do not drink...!" The third pass yields no touches, but Laertes, with a sudden, surprise cheap shot cuts Hamlet, revealing that Laertes has been fighting with an unbated blade! The two scuffle, and amid the confusion, Hamlet recovers Laertes' poisoned sword, wounding him, in turn, even as Queen Gertrude collapses from the wine!

The King's to Blame!

The comic effect of a single man flipping, quickly, from Hamlet to Claudius to Gertrude to Laertes is unavoidable, but here we seem to underline an already-present absurdity as all of these characters die in quick succession. In fact, I climax this series as Gertrude collapses and, rolling, transforms into Laertes, poisoned and lying on his side.

As mentioned, Laertes' turn in this crucial moment is probably made possible by Hamlet's previous apology. And the "j'accuse" climax of "The king! The king's to blame!" plays as the height of melodrama. (Even though Laertes is engaged in a one-on-one conversation with Hamlet, I cannot resist turning directly out to the audience at that crucial moment.)

"Envenomed too!" is a confirmation that Hamlet has **already** noticed that the point was "unbated." He is, in fact, so focused on his revenge that he seems almost not to have noticed that he, himself, is "slain." Instead, he sees his opening: Not only does he have a clean shot at the King with an "unbated" sword but, with Laertes accusation, it is clear that Claudius will die at the height of his wickedness, awash in the fresh guilt of three more murders: Gertrude, Hamlet and Laertes... (Could any revenge killing be more justified?)

As justified as it is, Hamlet (and I) cannot resist taking things over the top and, seeing the half-empty chalice still within arms' reach, I grab for it while grasping the King by the hair, pulling his head back up, pouring poison into his gaping jaw and flinging him, by that same hair, to the floor while howling: "follow my mother!"

Continuing to play all of the roles, I fling myself onto the floor, becoming Laertes, whose poisoned wound, we may assume, is deeper than Hamlet's cut, thus killing him more quickly, even though Hamlet was the first one wounded.

This "deathbed" exchange of forgiveness is crucial. We may recall that Hamlet's father, who died "with all my imperfections on my head" was suffering unspeakable torment in the afterlife. While we may not know the relative importance of Hamlet's other "sins": his relations with Ophelia ("be all my sins remembered"), his overweening pride ("playing God" while passing up his earlier opportunity to kill Claudius), or sending Rosencrantz and Guildenstern to "go to it," we are at least fairly certain that Claudius is headed for a much nastier place. (This is a very rare play in which the balance as measured in the afterlife, has been weighed ever-so-deliberately in the course of the resolution.)

Claudius offers up the lame excuse that Gertrude is swooning at the sight of the blood, but Gertrude, with her dying breath cries out, "The drink, the drink! I am poison'd."

Laertes, knowing that he too has been poisoned, turns informer...!

LAERTES
Hamlet, thou art slain;
No medicine in the world can do thee good;
...The treacherous instrument is in thy hand,
Unbated and envenom'd...
Thy mother's poison'd:
...The king, the king's to blame.

HAMLET
The point!--envenom'd too!
Then, venom, to thy work.
[Stabs KING CLAUDIUS.]
...Here, thou incestuous, murderous, damned Dane,
Drink off this potion. Is thy union here?
Follow my mother.

[CLAUDIUS dies.] Laertes asks:

LAERTES
Exchange forgiveness with me, noble Hamlet:
Mine and my father's death come not upon thee,
Nor thine on me. *[HE dies.]*

What a Wounded Name!

The indifference with which Hamlet tosses aside consideration of his mother's death sometimes gets a laugh. Of course, Hamlet is within seconds of his own death, but to cast her off without so much as a tear seems to level a final judgment on Gertrude's behavior: cheating on her husband, turning a blind eye to his murder, failing to properly mourn his death, marrying his brother, joining in on Claudius' drunken revelry and sexual exploits, and, what may nag Hamlet the most: probably returning to his bed after Hamlet has presented her with the full case against him. That is a much-too-tangled mess to untie in the final seconds of Hamlet's life, so "wretched Queen, adieu" will have to stand.

In fact it takes a back seat to Hamlet's much more pressing question: about to die with nothing ("since no man has aught of what he leaves") Hamlet wants to salvage the final thing that might actually matter to him in the Hereafter: his reputation. Were it not for Horatio (whose awareness of these intrigues may be traced back to Act I, Scene 1), Hamlet's death would seem like just one death amid some insane spree of unrighteous blood lust.

Let it Be.

Hamlet's "let it be" suggests that he is ready to die with the peace and balance suggested earlier in this act... as long as he has Horatio to make sense of this mess. Hamlet doesn't count on the astonishing loyalty that he seems to have inspired in his friend. Already having fallen to his knees on "this fell sergeant," Hamlet uses what is left of his strength to tear the cup from Horatio's hands. This time falling all the way to the floor, propped up only by his elbow for this final speech (emptying the cup as he speaks, so that Horatio will not be further tempted to kill himself).

In the midst of this devastation, Hamlet sees clearly enough to prophesy. **Deathbed prophecies in Shakespeare always come true** (at least when delivered by righteous characters). And while some might be tempted to play the pathos of the maudlin Hamlet losing everything in this final moment, I believe that Hamlet has achieved such balance and equanimity in these final scenes that he is, rather, struck by the irony of it all. Given that something is, after all, "rotten in the state of Denmark," perhaps the only way to cleanse the thing is to wipe the slate clean and have someone else take over. And struck, all of a sudden, by the ridiculous irony of all of this, I allow Hamlet a laugh in his dying moment, "on Fortinbras!"

As my staging proceeds, Hamlet rolls off of his elbow and onto his back for "The rest is silence," but continuing to roll upstage and onto my knees, I rise up again, this time as Horatio, holding and lowering the now-lifeless body of Hamlet on "Now cracks a noble heart," lifting his eyes above the audience as if seeing the spirit of his prince escorted away by "flights of angels."

HAMLET
Heaven make thee free of it! I follow thee.
I am dead, Horatio. Wretched queen, adieu!
You that look pale and tremble at this chance,
That are but mutes or audience to this act,
Had I but time--as this fell sergeant, death,
Is strict in his arrest--O, I could tell you--
But let it be. Horatio, I am dead;
Thou livest; report me and my cause aright
To the unsatisfied.

Horatio wants no more than to drink from the cup, and die alongside his prince.

HAMLET
Give me the cup: let go; by heaven, I'll have't.
O good Horatio, what a wounded name,
Things standing thus unknown, shall live behind me!
If thou didst ever hold me in thy heart
Absent thee from felicity awhile,
And in this harsh world draw thy breath in pain,
To tell my story.
O, I die, Horatio;
The potent poison quite o'er-crows my spirit:
I cannot live to hear the news from England;
But I do prophesy the election lights
On Fortinbras: he has my dying voice...
The rest is silence.
[Dies.]

HORATIO
Now cracks a noble heart. Good night sweet prince:
And flights of angels sing thee to thy rest!

Hamlet's Final Request

So far, we've kept Horatio's "voice" more or less out of the mix. I do quote him a few times, but largely in the tone and flow of my narrator's voice. And, of course, I let Hamlet interpret his own letters in Act IV, rather than having Horatio or Claudius read his words aloud. My intent is to reflect the surprise that I generally feel when I read this play and realize just how crucial of a character Horatio has been all along. His presence on-stage pre-dates Hamlet's first appearance, and post-dates his death, which leads us to view Hamlet through the eyes of his best friend. When Horatio seems shocked at the killing of Rosencrantz and Guildenstern, that shock resonates through us, giving us permission to see Hamlet in perspective. In an early speech from Act III (cut from this "breakneck" adaptation), Hamlet pays an endearing tribute to Horatio, further contrasting him from Rosencrantz and Guildenstern, who, we may recall, attempt to "play him like a pipe:"

> HAMLET
> For thou hast been
> As one, in suffering all, that suffers nothing,
> ...and blest are those
> Whose blood and judgment are so well commingled
> That they are not a pipe for fortune's finger
> To sound what stop she please. Give me that man
> That is not passion's slave, and I will wear him
> In my heart's core, ay, in my heart of heart,
> As I do thee.

As such, Horatio functions as a stand-in for the audience at large: poor in money, but rich in spirit.

When Horatio speaks up at last, we hear a pure voice, unembellished by the need to flatter his prince, but profoundly moved and tearful. And while we assume that most of Horatio's litany of the play's events, describing misdeeds of the late King ("carnal, bloody and unnatural" can only be describing Claudius), it may well be that "accidental judgments" and "casual slaughters" describe Hamlet's killing of Polonius and his dispatch of Rosencrantz and Guildenstern, respectively. I believe that Horatio, as **our** representative on the stage, hinting at criticism of the prince he clearly loves, informs us that we may admire Hamlet while remaining critical of those mistakes Hamlet made in the desperation of the moment.

And just as we met Horatio well in advance of meeting Hamlet, **even before meeting Horatio**, we were already aware of the state of fear that had been visited upon Denmark, confronted with the threat of troops led by Fortinbras. And so, it is only right that we "pan back out" one further level from Hamlet's story to re-introduce Fortinbras, and the larger consequence that this tale holds, not only for one man, but for the nation of Denmark.

The English Ambassadors arrive alongside Fortinbras and his company, disappointed to discover that their proud report that "Rosencrantz and Guildenstern are dead!"... *now falls on deaf ears. Horatio begins the seemingly impossible task of fulfilling on Hamlet's final request...*

HORATIO
And let me speak to the yet unknowing world
How these things came about: so shall you hear
Of carnal, bloody, and unnatural acts,
Of accidental judgments, casual slaughters,
Of deaths put on by cunning and forced cause,
And, in this upshot, purposes mistook
Fall'n on the inventors' heads.

Take up the bodies...

By this point of the play, a good many producers have already packed it in: the thing has stretched on for over 3½ hours, and with the death of our title character, there's nothing left to hold our interest but this dull sorting-out, as guards "take up the bodies" and Fortinbras takes over (a detail already anticipated and fed to us by the dying Hamlet). Why stick around? (Neither the Mel Gibson nor the Laurence Olivier "Hamlet" included Fortinbras at all!) Besides: Hamlet himself meets his end with the words "The rest is silence!"

I believe that Hamlet (the play) is bigger than Hamlet (the character). Our modern world, driven by a "cult of personality" (exacerbated by having Hollywood "stars" in the role), hangs on the crucial question of whether Hamlet lives or dies, and we are saddened by his death. We may even see it as a **flaw** of the play, that Shakespeare could not find a way to keep his hero alive. One attendee remarked, "That guy had a really rough day! And his girlfriend died!"

In the opening scene. Shakespeare put us into awareness of a country precariously threatened by an invasive force. In addition to this threat from without, Denmark continues to "rot" from within, and what is important about the deaths of Hamlet, Claudius, Gertrude, Polonius and Laertes is that these unnecessary deaths clear the way for Fortinbras to walk in and take over.

We want Hamlet to be about Hamlet, the character, but if we, the audience, have come to consider ourselves as local observers: fellow Danes who can observe the collapse of the royalty from a privileged vantage point, then the play is really about Denmark and the Danes and, by extension, about us. (Hamlet, who has been addressing us through much of this play, in these final moments calls us "mutes or audience to this act.") These five unnecessary deaths (six if we count the late King Hamlet) have wiped a nation of thousands... perhaps millions, clean of its leadership, rendering some imagined million people (ourselves amongst them) vulnerable to takeover, oppression, and perhaps slavery and death as a result of our leaders' envious intrigues.

We think that the stakes are about a **character** we have grown fond of through the course of a play. But, in point of fact, **we** are a portion of those stakes! I play this out to the end, entering as Fortinbras, speaking in the rich rounded vowels of a voice swollen with power, ordering soldiers about, sneering distastefully at the human wreckage at my feet, and, for the first time through this entire presentation, sitting authoritatively on the throne. (Neither Claudius nor Hamlet have had the time to actually **occupy** the ever-present throne.) Fortinbras scans the crowd of his new subjects, richly satisfied, contemplating his future as the new king, as the lights go down and the music swells.

And we, perhaps, wonder whether we are in the command of a benevolent leader or a tyrant.

Fortinbras, the last prince left standing, claims the throne without a shot being fired.

PRINCE FORTINBRAS
...Let four captains
Bear Hamlet, like a soldier, to the stage;
For he was likely, had he been put on,
To have proved most royally...
Take up the bodies: such a sight as this
Becomes the field, but here shows much amiss.

Also available from TMRT Press…! And on tour…!
Molière Than Thou

Best of Fringe: Best Adapted Work.   *San Francisco Fringe Festival*

The audience is enthralled… Timothy Mooney is the real deal… A very tight performance indeed, which should be seen by any aspiring actor who wants to tread the boards.   *George Psillidies, nytheatre.com*

"Top Ten of 2006" One-of-a-kind… original, weird and seriously funny… one of the most creative and refreshing pieces of classical theatre I've seen in years… Mooney's translations make Molière's 17th century language instantly accessible. His interpretations were crisp, stylized and sang with the comic genius of the playwright's original intent. *Ruth Cartlidge, Chattanooga Pulse*

Mooney is clearly enraptured by the great French playwright… The translations are wonderful… well worth seeing. *Amy Barratt, Montreal Mirror*

The humanities are in safe hands this year.   *San Francisco Bay Guardian*

Molière has never been more accessible…   *Marie J. Kilker, aislesay.com*

Outstanding… A number of patrons found the performance too short, because they could have listened to Mr. Mooney all day.   *Ken Gordon, CBC*

The listener can draw all the available pleasure from the splendid speeches penned by the French Shakespeare.   *Kevin Prokosh, Winnipeg Free Press*

Clearly Molière lives.   *Elizabeth Maupin, Orlando Sentinel*

A must-see for aspiring drama students and a pleasant experience for the rest of us…   *The Vue Weekly, Edmonton*

I highly recommend his skilled impersonation of one of the theater's most gifted and important creative spirits.   *Al Krulik, Orlando Weekly*

If you're not passionate about Molière now, you may well be at the end of the show…   *Marianne Hales Harding – Seattle Fringe Fest Review Rag*

One of the reasons that Molière's work has survived is that, sadly, his enemies have outlived him… But what he left us were his vast quantity of words… articulate, brilliant, hilarious, disgusting, despairing… We need his voice. And he's funny as hell.   *Minnesota Fringe Blogger, Phillip Low*

TMRT Press, PO Box 638, Prospect Heights, IL 60070 * www.timmooneyrep.com

Also Available from TMRT Press!

Acting at the Speed of Life; *Conquering Theatrical Style*

A unique, refreshing and highly practical approach… No nonsense steps to approach the demands of stylized acting… This exceedingly valuable book will inspire actors to approach stylized theatre with the spirit of fun and style.
James Fisher, Theatre Library Association's "Broadside"

Author Timothy Mooney takes on the challenges of asides, soliloquies and rhetorical speech. He offers tips on memorizing lines, incorporating the "stuff" of historical style, and going beyond naturalism and realism as it suits the playwright's intent. Nicely done. *Stage Directions Magazine*

A gem of a book that demystifies the acting process by mixing common-sense instruction with practical exercises. It ought to have a place on every actor's and director's bookshelf. Not that it ought to stay there. Keep it handy for audition preparation, classroom studies, rehearsals and sometimes simply for a good read… He inspires his readers with a clear common-sense approach, eye-opening analyses of familiar texts, and wise advice that encourages newcomers and veteran actors to grow into the best they can be.
Michael Howley, Southern Theatre

Terrific… Replete with incisive, clear-headed accessible advice… The clearest and most comprehensive work for the community and student actor written today. *Dr. Christian H. Moe, Southern Illinois University*

Not just your average acting book: A comprehensive understanding of the basic skills needed to survive. Powerful and empowering… it's necessary for every serious actor's shelf. *Dennis Wemm, Glenville State College*

The hardest-working book in my life of teaching acting to high school students… From the basics of memorization to the clearing of the cobwebs surrounding the classics, the book does it all with grace and great humor.
Claudia Haas, Playwright for Youth/Artist in Residence, Twin Cities

A thunderous success! My cabaret class came alive with interpretive freedom. *Loren F. Salter, Artistic Director and Performance Coach*

Probably the most accessible approach to classical style that I have ever seen.
Celi Oliveto, Master of Letters/MFA Candidate, Mary Baldwin College

This could be the modern manual for the Director and the Actor.
Charley Ault, Director, Players Guild of the Festival Playhouse

NO other book I've read captures these simple tasks that are so important.
Janice Fronczak, University of Nebraska-Kearney

TMRT Press, PO Box 638, Prospect Heights, IL 60070 * www.timmooneyrep.com

If you enjoyed this book...

- You may want to share it with friends, teach it in your classes, or get copies for your library...
- You may want to stage it with your students or theatre company...
- You may want to share your own reactions, thoughts and stories with the author...
- You may want to follow Tim's exploits, read his blog, or learn of other works available from TMRT Press, such as *Shakespeare's Histories, Acting at the Speed of Life, The Big Book of Molière Monologues, Molière than Thou* or *Criteria, a One-Man Comic Sci-Fi Thriller!*

If so, please go to **www.timmooneyrep.com** for lots of fun stuff, including links to blog, video, scripts and bookings for *Breakneck Hamlet, Shakespeare's Histories, Lot o' Shakespeare, Molière than Thou* and *The Greatest Speech of All Time!*

Or, you can fill out the form below, and send it with your order for more copies of the book to:

TMRT Press
c/o Timothy Mooney
P.O. Box 638
Prospect Heights, IL 60070

You can also send your thoughts, comments and stories to this address. Tim loves reading your feedback, input and adventures!

Name _____

Address _____

City, State, Zip _____

Telephone _____

E-mail address _____

I would like to order _____ copies of "_____"!
I would like info for ordering multiple copies for school or library use! ❑
I would also like to be on the list for Tim's Blog! ❑
I would like to talk about licensing this play for production! ❑
Other comments and thoughts (use additional pages, if necessary):

_____

_____

_____

Thank you for your enthusiasm!
Tim Mooney

Made in the USA
San Bernardino, CA
29 September 2015